# PROPHET
## OR TRAITOR?

## The Jimmy Hogan Story

GW00645013

**The Parrs Wood Press**
<u>Manchester</u>

**First Published 2003**

**THE PARRS WOOD PRESS**
St Wilfrid's Enterprise Centre
Royce Road, Manchester, M15 5BJ
www.parrswoodpress.com


© Norman Fox 2003


**ISBN: 1 903158 45 1**


Printed by Newton Printing Ltd of London
www.newtonprinting.com

For an unswerving supporter...Gill

# CONTENTS

# ABOUT THE AUTHOR

Norman Fox is one of Britain's most experienced sports journalists. His career began in the late 1950s on local newspapers in Kent before spending several years with World Sports magazine. He joined The Times in 1966 and remained with the paper for twenty-three years, starting as a sub-editor and finishing as Deputy Managing Editor. At various times he was Football Correspondent (1976-1980, in succession to the master of football writers, Geoffrey Green), Athletics Correspondent and General Sports Correspondent (1980-82), Sports Editor (1982-86), Deputy Managing Editor (1986-89). He was then invited to become the first Football Correspondent of the new Independent on Sunday for whom he continues to freelance. He has reported four Olympic Games, several football World Cup final competitions as well as all the major domestic and European finals, World and European athletics championships and a wide range of motor sports events. He is married with two daughters and recently moved back to Whitstable, where he was born, and where he began his journalistic career.

# ACKNOWLEDGEMENTS

The author is particularly grateful to the following: Ms Frankie Hogan, John Hogan, Chris Riding, Denis De M. Guilfoyle LVO OBE, The late Philip Guilfoyle.

Many people enthusiastically came forward to offer their memories of time spent with Jimmy Hogan or provided helpful information: Ron Atkinson, Denis Bennett, Gary Broughton, Paul Cain, Christine Carradice (Nelson Library), Mr. A. Cheetham, Barry Cragg, Tommy Docherty, Alex Farmer, Alf Fields, Ken Friar OBE, Brian Glanville, John Gleeson, Mr. N. Hudson, Edward Lee (Burnley Express), John McKerrol, Peter McParland, Robin Michel, Peter Ogden, Olav Ouwerkerk (Dordrecht 90 Football Club), Jim Pollard, Ken Roberts, Johnny Paton, Mrs. J.Pollard, Neil Rioch (Chairman, Aston Villa Former Players' Association), Ray Simpson (Honorary Historian and Statistician, Burnley Football Club), John Whittaker.

The author would like to thank the following people and organisations for the use of photographic material: The Hogan family, Hulton Getty Archive and the Illustrated London News.

# TRIBUTES

*We have built upon the results of his work and therefore owe him a great deal.*
**Hans Passblack**
(Secretary General, German Football-Federation)

*He taught us everything we know about football.*
**Sandor Barcs**
(President of the Hungarian Football Association)

*He was a shining example for the coaching profession.*
**Helmut Schoen**
(West German team manager)

*You talk about people being ahead of their time - well he was certainly that.*
**Ron Atkinson**

*I have heard Sir Matt Busby referred to as the Father of Football. Jimmy Hogan deserves a share in that title.*
**Tommy Docherty**

*The most remarkable coach produced by any country in the history of the game.*
**Brian Glanville**

*The greatest coach football has ever known.*
**Len Shackleton**

# INTRODUCTION

WITH THE MEMORABLE EXCEPTION OF 1966, when Alf Ramsey's inspiring leadership and tactical pragmatism resulted in England's unremarkable but cleverly motivated and patriotic team winning the World Cup on home ground, the birthplace of organised football so consistently failed to make a truly significant impact on what had grown into the world's most popular sport that the Football Association finally turned, in desperation, to a foreign coach, the Swede Sven Goran Eriksson. In the World Cup of 2002 he did well to take England as far as the quarter-finals, including a notable victory against Argentina. Yet when they came up against Brazil, who by their own high standards were not an outstanding side and played the last part of the game with ten men, they again lacked the skill to grasp the opportunity. It was a familiar story.

When and why did English football at international level go wrong? Each successive manager of the national team has given his opinion on the question Why? A common theme has been that domestic competition is too demanding. In reality it requires little more in terms of the number of matches played than elsewhere in Europe. The unyielding pace of the average English league game has been offered as another reason. Certainly the speed of most Premiership matches is often unrelentingly high, but the physical demands on the players are no greater than in many other sports and less than in athletics and cycling, which is as well since those sports have been discredited by infinitely more drug abuse than is believed to be the case in football.

The answer to Why? is linked with When? It goes back a long time but remains the strongest clue to enduring failure. English international football's post-Second World War disappointments are rooted in a sad, illogical lack of trust in the value of real skill, but the poisonous seed need never have taken hold had the game's administrators and the clubs themselves taken heed of the warnings so often dispensed by the man the Press of the time called 'Football's Forgotten Genius'.

Jimmy Hogan was never properly recognised in his own country and as a result became the brain behind a sporting Hungarian revolution which later led to Continental countries placing England on the sidelines of the world game. He was also credited with inspiring the rise of German football and, together with the astute manager Hugo Meisl, he guided the Austrian 'Wunderteam' that in the early 1930s gave the previously self-assured England and the domestic game's insular leaders what should have been the fright of their lives.

This is the story of a determined but often mistrusted Lancastrian of Irish lineage. Many of football's most famous names, past and present, have said he could have put England on a path that would have avoided so many of her national teams being left behind and sometimes humiliated. In his prime, when he was one of the Continent's most successful trainer-coaches, he was never offered the opportunity to come back home on a permanent basis and use his talents to prepare English football at international level for the challenge of a changing game. As a result he spent most of his career making foreign countries and clubs ready for the time when they would leave England languishing in the second division of international football. One day, one match, one defeat finally proved how wrong football in his home country had been to spurn the opportunity to profit from his uncommon skills.

# 1

# The Castle Crumbles

ENGLAND'S POSITION AS the most powerful nation in world football had long been on borrowed and often disputed time, but even going into the second half of the 20th century the national team still retained the distinction of never having lost on home soil. A 2-0 defeat by the Republic of Ireland on Everton's ground in 1949 had always been dismissed as not counting since the Irish were not really 'foreigners'. The record ended on November 25, 1953, a murky, momentous day at Wembley stadium. The indignity of losing to Hungary was compounded by the magnitude of the defeat: 6-3. England had already lost their invincibility when playing abroad but on that afternoon the world also became aware that as far as football was concerned an Englishman's home was no longer his castle. The overwhelming victory was inflicted by a country freely admitting that it would never have happened but for the work of Jimmy Hogan, a single-minded, obsessive coach to whom all of Hungary's officials and players dedicated their triumph. Their manager-coach, Gusztav Sebes, said: "No single match in the whole of English sporting history has caused such interest as this one. We played football as Jimmy Hogan taught us. When our soccer history is told, his name should be written in gold letters."

Sandor Barcs, who led the Hungarian delegation, was asked how his country's victory had come about. He said, simply:

# PROPHET OR TRAITOR?

"You had better go back thirty years to the time your Jimmy Hogan came to teach us how to play. Am I rude if I say England could, with advantage, use some of the hints he gave us? He taught us everything we know about football." Rude? If truth be told, that same remark could have been repeated after any number of indifferent, physically tough but skill-deprived England performances seen in half a century of international football since 1953.

On that grey winter day in the "Celebration Year" of the Coronation, which also saw the first climbing of Everest and the Matthews' Cup Final, Hogan, a spry 70-year-old, took his seat at Wembley certain and troubled that he was about to see something to deflate his country's nationalistic pride. Legend has it that he was in the Royal Box as the Hungarian Football Association's Guest of Honour. Actually, he had talked Aston Villa into buying a few tickets and organising a coach to take him and some of the young Villa players - who, in spite of his age he was still coaching - to the most consequential match in England's long football history.

He was not even invited by the Football Association or the Hungarian federation to the official post-match banquet. Some FA committee members must have spotted him in the stands close to the VIP seats and been aware that this was the man English international football had rejected but who now had returned, white-haired and haunting, to witness its most damning condemnation of everything that had gone wrong and everything he had foretold would happen. Hardly any wonder that some of them viewed him as a traitor because he had not only planted the tap-root of the Hungarian football that so humbled England, but had done similar work in Germany, the old enemy in football as well as war.

The match against Hungary was both the proudest yet most harrowing experience of his life. When the Hungarians realised their mistake in not inviting him to the official match-day

# THE CASTLE CRUMBLES

function, they pleaded with him to attend the following day's celebratory cocktail party in London. He had to make a difficult decision: whether to go and enjoy the praise of those who probably would not have had cause to celebrate without the work he had done years before, or dispel any feelings of personal guilt by returning to the Villa training pitch where several of the boys he had taken to Wembley would surely be asking how they could emulate the players who in the morning papers were dubbed the "Magic Magyars".

He fought with his indecision and finally followed the path of loyalty. It lay with the youngsters who were the future of English football which he had so wanted to help long before it was in such need. He told the Hungarians: "On Thursday I always coach the junior players." His dedication to responsibility took precedence over his lifelong yearning to be recognised as one of the greatest coaches of all time, but doubtless it was a close-run thing.

The English FA members were mortified by Hungary's overwhelming victory and disconcerted by Hogan's presence at Wembley. Their team had been so completely outplayed that towards the end of his life the captain, Billy Wright, admitted that thoughts of the defeat could still give him restless nights. He confessed that it was not an exaggeration to say that some of those FA officials "probably considered Hogan a traitor". He, perhaps more than anyone in the beaten team, recognised that the Hungarians had shown just how far English football had fallen behind the march of the best Continental countries. He recalled: "I knew then that they were playing a different game to us. We had to start a revolution in our own game."

Some of the FA committee acknowledged that in the years before and immediately after the First World War, no other trainer-coach had contributed as much to the growth of the game in Europe as Hogan. But what they could not admit was that failure to give him sufficient opportunities to teach in his home country had, unforgivably, contributed to England's downfall. That, though, was just as much the fault of the clubs who placed little or no emphasis on coaching.

A long line of committee-men in charge of the destiny of English football at national level and most of the men who controlled the clubs had been myopic to the fact that Hogan and his coaching methods, which emphatically placed skill above physical power and had been the foundation of the football uprising in Europe, could have saved the country not only from the indignities of 1953 and 1954 (England lost the return match in Budapest 7-1) but, with the exception of the 1966 victory, would possibly have avoided the long series of World Cup failures that finally led to the admission that no Englishman was good enough to coach his own country.

As one of Hogan's grandsons, Chris Riding, remarked: "With due respect to Sven Goran Eriksson, grandfather would have turned in his grave." England, he said, had treated Hogan as an "eccentric" who was even criticised by Stanley Rous, an innovator and distinguished administrator. Hogan, Rous suggested, was too secretive about his coaching technique, too full of his own importance and barely employable at a national level. Hungary, Austria, France, Holland and Germany had thought otherwise.

After the match at Wembley the old man tried not to show emotion but he was in turmoil. He had been born and raised in Lancashire. He particularly loved Burnley and returned there to retire. Indeed, he spent his last months within the sound of a goal being scored at Turf Moor. He confessed that England's defeat made him feel deep misgivings since he was all too aware that in many eyes what he had done for Continental football did indeed verge on treachery. But, with equal intensity, he carried a lasting resentment for never having been given the credit in England for his achievements, nor having the opportunity to take responsibility for the national team long before 1946 when the FA reluctantly backed down a little with their policy of selection by committee and appointed Walter Winterbottom as the national team's first full-time coach. It was Winterbottom who was still in charge of England on that defining day in 1953, but his hands remained tied by the stiff, pedantic, largely elderly guardians of FA policy.

Hungary's victory led to relentless inquests in the Press. Winterbottom was criticised for his failure to make tactical changes during the match but it was widely acknowledged that he had been a victim of the FA's failure to give him sufficient control over the preparation of the team. Even so, many writers and people involved at club level urged that in spite of his age Hogan should take over, or at least be taken on in an advisory role alongside Winterbottom. After all, he had first-hand experience of the way the Hungarians had originally been schooled in the football that had made England look old-fashioned. Who else was better qualified?

Still amazingly fit and able to perform the skills he taught, Hogan himself felt sure that age was no impediment, but the FA used it as the main reason to maintain the status quo. Winterbottom remained and, to his lasting credit, he did a huge amount to encourage coaching. Eventually, though, the FA turned to Alf Ramsey who brought England the World Cup, at some cost to imaginative and free-spirited football. Hogan celebrated the 1966 victory but only as a patriot. He deplored its consequences. He was not alone. Undoubtedly Ramsey raised the spirits of the people of England but at the same time the victory sent out a false message which suggested that direct, never-say-die football, often played without wingers, was the way forward. It may not have been his intention. He could only work with the material available, and he did that better than anyone before or since.

Hogan's visit to Wembley in 1953 had brought such a range of feelings that towards the end of his life he said it was an experience that might have been better had he "watched the match from above". It was no off-the-cuff remark. He was profoundly religious. He never had a whisper of doubt that there was an after-life. Often, though, he wondered whether football was too "earthy" to have any place in his idea of heaven, or even if he had been wrong to get involved in the game in the first place. After all, heaven without football would have been his definition of hell.

He could understand that at Wembley there was ill-feeling amongst some of football's most influential voices but at the same time he was proud to have been offered the opportunity to teach the Hungarians in their formative years, as well as having the chance to show many other European national and club teams how to play in a way he felt had been spurned by English and, particularly, Scottish football after the earlier years of valuing ball control and intelligent passing. It was not that he thought British players lacked ability, only that they were poorly led. He always maintained that the British Isles produced the most natural footballers in the northern hemisphere, but that they were too often left without guidance as the game in the rest of the world changed direction away from endurance and towards the skillful control of the ball and the free movement of players uninhibited by old-fashioned positional and tactical restrictions. In later years the philosophy would be called "Total Football". He was teaching a version of it more than twenty years before Franz Beckenbauer and Johan Cruyff were born.

Before they returned to Budapest many of the Hungarian visitors to Wembley reiterated what had been said about Hogan, but it was Sebes who summarised all of their feelings by remarking: "Jimmy prepared the earth that brought about the flowering of Continental football." Hogan himself should have known that he had no reason to feel guilty about doing so much to bring about the time when England were finally beaten in their homeland. It was not as if he had not repeatedly warned everyone in his own country that the day would come. He had said it and written it so often that the only conclusion had to be that amongst the game's most senior councillors and at club level there were many deliberately deaf ears and anchors against progress.

Without a doubt he would rather have taught British players how to be ready for the Continental challenge than eventually listen to the Hungarian's praising him for England's downfall which, after all, had been predicted not only by himself but the country's more astute football commentators. "A lot of people offered me their congratulations," he said, "but I was very sad. After all I was a British coach and for over twenty years working all over Europe I had always fought for the prestige of British football. I was proud to see my old pupils give such a display, but it was still a shock to see England defeated." He told Sebes: "That was the kind of football that I dreamed the Hungarians might one day be able to play." He added that he had long been saying that English football had become far too dependent on strength and stamina at the expense of the skills that had once made the national team unbeatable.

In the weeks that followed, the concerted Press campaign continued to implore the FA to give him some responsibility for improving coaching at national level. The idea was enthusiastically supported by the public but the FA refused to acknowledge the mood of the country and would not countenance his employment, even in an advisory capacity. Several of the most famous players of the time said that this was a moment when England needed to seek the unique experience of a man who could ensure that in spite of the defeat by Hungary, England might still retain a permanent place among the top half dozen footballing countries of the world.

# PROPHET OR TRAITOR?

Inevitably, the Press described him a "prophet without honour in his own land". Fans across the country had been awoken to what English football at international level had missed. Hogan himself explained his thinking in a short televised interview. He spoke of the need to remember that football was a game in which skill ought to be encouraged far more than it had been in the era before England's Wembley debacle. That brought him a small mountain of letters. Most of the writers thanked him for pointing out why England had gone wrong. A small minority told him to get back to the Continent since it was, in their opinion, only a traitor who would be praised for creating the source of Hungary's mischief.

It would be difficult to imagine anyone in football's international history having such divided loyalties as he suffered when England were forced to question long-held beliefs. The amateur administrators could no longer brush the warnings aside. Defeats abroad - and there had been many - could always be put down to local conditions, the heat, the poor pitches and the tiredness of players who had been involved in the tough domestic programme. Now there were no more excuses. Admittedly, the team chosen to play against the Hungarians had some flaws but that was not the point. The presumed pupils had not only beaten the teachers but outwitted them tactically and with ball control that in the English league had once been prized but since almost disregarded

While Hogan loyally continued to maintain that potentially Britain still had the best players in the world, clearly the style of playing had gone badly wrong and the training methods were, as he said, "seriously at fault". In contemporary language, England had failed to realise that they were involved in a "whole new ball game".

The Hungarians said it was purely an administrative oversight in the preparations for the historic match at Wembley that led to their failure to make Hogan Guest of Honour. Not being given to false modesty, he never disabused those who spread the story that he was the principal invitee. In reality he never moved from his seat amongst the small group of novice Villa players who were under his tuition. In an article written for the Evening Despatch in Birmingham a few months after the match he said: "Those youngsters of mine asked many questions during the international game. They absorbed everything. So much so that on the following Saturday in an away game they played brilliantly." They had been so impressed with this seemingly ancient teacher, who could still dribble past them and nine times out of ten hit a bucket with the ball from ten yards, that they had gone along with him to London curious but dubious about his repeated promise that they would almost certainly witness something out of the ordinary. They were not disappointed, at least with the standard of football performed by the Hungarians - a standard to which Hogan immediately insisted they should aspire. They were mightily disappointed with England.

Six months after their win at Wembley the Hungarians did indeed compensate Hogan for their omission in London. They feted him as a hero and found it difficult to understand why he was not overjoyed when Hungary's huge second victory in Budapest became the biggest thrashing in English football's ninety-year international history. The Daily Express reporter wrote: "Billy Wright came off with his face as white as his shirt, and looking like a man who has seen a ghost come back to haunt him. As hard as this giant-hearted man tried, he could not get near to suppressing the irrepressible Puskas." Hogan himself was clearly embarrassed by the outcome.

In spite of seeing the Hungarians twice confirm all of his warnings about their potential and England's falling standards, on neither occasion did he have any doubt about his life-long patriotism. "I had worked in so many countries that my family became known as the 'football circus'," he would say. "But my

# PROPHET OR TRAITOR?

only real home was in England…and Lancashire." He was also proud of his Irishness but his love of England was rivalled by only three things: football, which consumed him to the point of fixation, the Roman Catholic church, to which he was unswervingly devoted, and his family who had to become accustomed to a nomadic existence.

Religion dictated his attitude and the direction of his life. It was such a strong pilot that many of those who came in contact with him said he set standards of morality that in the rough world of football were impossible to follow and left many of them feeling that, not only in football terms but ethically, he was an unrealistic taskmaster. Those who did take his guidance without reservation did so with something approaching the devotion of disciples. Among them was Tommy Docherty, the Celtic, Preston, Arsenal, Chelsea and Scotland wing half who later became manager of, amongst other clubs, Manchester United. He said Hogan was "without doubt" the most important influence not only on his career but his life.

Docherty was appalled that football turned its back on someone who was proud yet remorseful to have been associated with the cause of the English game's most damning moments. He knew that the effective, stylish, ball mastery of the "Magic Magyars" had evolved from Hogan's own highly individualistic teaching skill which had been accepted on the Continent in the years when British football was all-powerful and saw no shadows creeping towards its future.

During his time abroad Hogan collected any number of medals struck for him by foreign clubs in recognition of his work, yet when he occasionally returned to England his bitterness at a lack of acknowledgment (doubtless combined with not particularly well concealed vanity) persuaded him to scrawl his autograph "Jimmy Hogan - The World's Number One Coach". He always needed to remind anyone who would listen that he was a successful football missionary with little credit in his own country while in Hungary he was known with affection and appreciation as "Jimmy Bacsi" (Uncle Jimmy).

After England's defeats and before Wolverhampton Wanderers courageously but misleadingly diverted attention away from domestic football's deficiencies with their dramatic 3-2 friendly defeat of a less than fully-committed Honved - who included Puskas and several other members of the victorious Hungarian national team - the British Press would regularly ask him for his opinions and praise him for his achievements (most of which had largely gone without mention before 1953). For many of the writers, the approbation came only with the benefit of hindsight. Because of the country's insularity, its unswerving belief in English football's superiority and a particularly cynical attitude towards coaching, in the end it pleaded too late to grasp the last years of his life. The Continent had long been receptive to his ideas and his commitment. Suddenly English football wanted and needed to forgive itself for not doing the same.

The full significance of England's first home defeat cannot be underestimated. England not only lost their home invincibility. The whole team and all of the football writers of the day were left with the thought that the defeat could have been even worse. The gap in skill could be measured not in goals but years. For the Continentals, their time had come and the Hungarians knew to whom, more than anyone, they needed to offer their thanks. The football of Puskas, Hidegkuti, Kocsis and the rest was born several decades before. It emerged from the mind and experience of an unlikely source.

# 2

# "The Parson"

HOGAN'S LOVE OF FOOTBALL was not inherited. His parents were always too involved with bringing up a large family to have time or money for much recreation. Without knowing it at the time, his determination to control a football was to allow him to have command over his own destiny. He would spend hour upon solitary hour working on his skills. None of his mates had such single-minded patience nor, above all, his resolute self-belief. Throughout his life he would turn most conversations towards his favourite subjects: his own career, his opinion that football was a game demanding skill that might come naturally to some but could always be improved even amongst the stars of the game, and his religion.

If a proportion of the boys and men he later coached were to find him a slightly disconcerting, curious mix of kindly character and almost impossibly demanding perfectionist, others, including some of the finest players and coaches of the twentieth century, said that he was the most important guide on their journeys through football. Hungary's Gusztav Sebes maintained that his own career was significantly motivated by his studying of the work of all the most distinguished coaches and managers, not least the Italian Vittorio Pozzo, English football's Herbert Chapman and Austria's Hugo Meisl, without whom Hogan himself would never have been given his opportunities. However, he added that the greatest credit was due to Hogan.

# "THE PARSON"

If, eventually, football offered Hogan the means to live a life of adventure that because of a tough upbringing he never thought likely, the Roman Catholic church challenged him to live that life within its strictest rules of behaviour. At the same time he had to mix with a breed of men with little regard for his dogmatic ethics. Few who worked with him found it easy to follow the guidelines that were, to him, essential to the way he wanted to live. He embraced the principles with such complete assurance that they shaped his lifestyle, his personality and, for better or worse, his relationships with everyone with whom he associated, from fellow professionals to his own family.

Not without good reason would some of the players he coached nickname him 'The Parson'. Swearing, presumed then as now endemic in the game, was virtually unknown in his company, and those players who joined him at Mass were probably more likely to be forgiven their trespasses on the field and in training than those who did not.

There is little doubt that his father, James, would have preferred to see his son go into the priesthood rather than live a wandering life in football. And, briefly, in the natural ferment of teenage years, Jimmy was slightly torn between a career amongst crude-talking professional footballers and the Church. While the Church promised greater security, football offered the better pay, though only marginally, and he was never one to underestimate the importance of a good day's wage for a hard day's work. Poverty had driven his family from Ireland to Lancashire where his father had found work in Bradford's cotton industry. In the mill James met Margaret O'Donnell whose family had come from County Mayo for similar reasons. When he was offered a better job with more money as a foreman dyer, James married Margaret and moved to Nelson. But when Jimmy was born, on October 16, 1882, life in Victoria Street was still far from comfortable.

# PROPHET OR TRAITOR?

The terrace house was often cold in winter and stiflingly crowded all year. As well as his parents, there was Jimmy's grandfather on his father's side and a woman lodger who helped look after the eleven children (reflecting on those times he would often say "we were a complete team") until they were old enough to go to work in the mills, which for girls meant starting when they were only eleven. The eldest of his sisters, Ellen, made clear what the other children must have been thinking. What the family really needed, she said, was not another baby but a horse and cart. Another mouth to feed when more often than not there was insufficient bread in the house seemed to her absurd, but it was typical of the times.

Ironically, in view of his sister's thoughts about bread, her new brother was baptised at the local Corn Exchange, which was used as the Catholic Church before a real one was built. Until the family moved to Burnley, when Jimmy was eight, he attended St. Joseph's School, where religious education was considered just as important as reading, writing and arithmetic.

Burnley was to become what it is tempting to call his spiritual home, though he himself would never have used the term since his spiritual needs were served in full by whatever church he happened to attend, wherever he happened to be, anywhere he travelled or lived. But Burnley was lastingly dear to him, a place to which over the years he returned time and again: a place that had a famous and successful League football club for which in the eager time of his youth he had dreams of playing.

When he was old enough for secondary education at St. Mary Magdalene's School, he was thinking less about what the teachers expected of him than dwelling on his own anticipation of getting back on to the street to spend every spare minute kicking tin cans, home-made balls made of rags, or wooden ones picked up from behind the coconut shy at visiting local fairs. Walking home one day he saw an old hat in the road and instinctively kicked it, not knowing that it had been placed in waiting for a football-mad kid like him. Under the hat was a large stone. He crushed his toes and for several weeks it seemed that he might never walk properly again, let alone play football. It was six months before he could run.

After his recovery his skill kicking any sort of ball or bunch of rags became so good that his mates began to call him "The Pro". In later years he liked to tell anyone who would listen that the nickname was prophetic because when he went abroad to become a full-time trainer the calling card he had printed described himself as "Football Professor". Brilliant teacher though he was, such a desire to be respected told of a deep anger. Back in Britain a full-time football coach, let alone a self-styled "Professor", was not considered necessary even to the biggest clubs in the land.

Because of his strict upbringing he was haunted by any suspicion of wrong doing and, touchingly, even in his eighties, he would still recall an incident in childhood which for a teenager in the ill-disciplined 21st century would be forgotten within the hour, and certainly not something to be regretted for a lifetime. On the way to and from school he and his friends would kick their wooden ball from one side of the street to the other, avoiding the steam trams that rattled down the middle. On one occasion he kicked it further than he intended. It went straight to the feet of a young policeman. The boys waited. Each one expected a reprimand but the policeman was of like mind and kicked it back, except that his aim was not as good as most of the schoolboys and it went straight through a shop window. Hogan and his friends ran off, with the young constable joining them in escaping before anyone noticed. Hogan said he felt full of remorse. He should have stopped and taken the blame. He considered the episode was his fault because he was not accurate enough with his own kick.

# PROPHET OR TRAITOR?

He was only ten when his infant skill was first noticed by anyone apart from his own mates and offended schoolmasters, who saw him as a naturally bright child and thought he should have been concentrating on more important things. A salesman who had been at the school selling books stopped to watch him juggling with a ball in the playground and called him over to compliment him on his ability while at the same time offering him a halfpenny, the largest amount of money he had ever been given. For the rest of his days he said that was the moment he "turned professional".

In spite of being small for his age, he was competitive and, more to the point, able to control any sort of ball with almost mysterious domination. He played his first semi-organised matches for his church team and spent every available moment, often on his own, developing his natural ability by practising in the small backyard, in the streets or on the ash surfaces of the local recreation grounds: Gannow Top, Hargher Clough and Fulledge. He would often say that he was a product of "the Burnley rec., football, clogs and all," adding, "and if you can control a ball on cinders, wearing clogs, you can call yourself a footballer."

He was eleven-years-old before he played a proper match on a grass pitch. At last he could aim his shots between real goalposts rather than a pile of clothes. The opportunity had come only because his father gained further promotion at the mill and was at last sufficiently well off to send him to St. Bede's College, Manchester. There, playing on fine, smooth pitches at Whalley Range, and in spite of stiff competition from boys who came from the hot-beds of football - Manchester, Liverpool, Preston, Bolton and Blackburn - he became captain of the first team at football, captain of cricket and, to prove that he had some academic ability, captain of the school itself. In his first appearance for the First XI he scored the winning goal and was chaired off by the rest of the side. He was to make a habit of performing brilliantly in debut games.

# "THE PARSON"

Football always dominated his thinking but his thoughts began to move on from simple day-dreaming about the chances of becoming a full-time player. He was beginning to consider tactics and the need to have complete mastery over the ball in whatever circumstance he might find himself on the pitch. After leaving school he played for St. Mary's Church team which was almost entirely Irish. In his first and only season with them they remained unbeaten until the middle of March when, with bizarre irony since they were all wearing sprigs of shamrock, they lost their record on St Patrick's Day. By then he was sixteen and with the naïve confidence of his young years he went down to Burnley's ground and demanded a trial. Surprisingly, he was given one for his nerve but asked to hold back on his ambitions by the manager, Ernest Magnall, who said he thought he had talent but was not ready. Never lacking confidence, he told Magnall: "I feel sure that I can play better than many of the men I have seen in your practice matches."

At the same time he had been spotted by Burnley Belvedere, who played in the powerful Lancashire Amateur League. Having been reasonably good at "numbers" at school, he was also articled to a Burnley accountant. Actually he had much preferred geography to arithmetic and would spend his evenings leafing through an old atlas wondering whether he would ever get to visit far-off countries. Football turned him into one of the most travelled men of his times.

He knew that he was not natural office material but he was certainly an intuitive inside-forward. Although he had been scoring goals, he was not big enough to lead the attack. Nor was he sufficiently tough to be a wing half or defender. He had the sort of delicate skill that in England then and for years afterwards was often met with the impatient cry of "Get rid of it!". The ball-holding and thoughtful ingenuity of inside forwards, from Hogan through to Len Shackleton, Tommy Harmer, Alan Hudson, Tony Currie, Glenn Hoddle and too many more to mention, has never been completely trusted by managers, especially those who have had the unenviable job of being in charge of England. Special ball skills in English players have, for generations, been considered dangerous luxuries and too often rejected as being self-indulgent.

It was the lack of recognition for what he considered to be the most essential and entertaining part of the game (holding the ball within his confident and much-rehearsed control) that irked him from an early age and eventually drove him into making a career in countries where everything he believed to be important was recognised and worked upon with relentless enthusiasm.

His father had driven himself to exhaustion to raise the large family but money was still tight. While with Burnley Belvedere Jimmy was embarrassed because most of the other players came from much better off families. Some were even the sons of the local mill owners who could help pay for travel expenses and the general maintenance of the club whereas the club itself had to subsidise him because he was earning less than a shilling a week. Perhaps that was a hint as to why, when he was later seen to be a player of interesting ability, his career was frequently frustrated by arguments about money.

Whether through lack of recognition or his own failure to convince when it mattered, his time as a player, which lasted for fourteen seasons, never matched the success he would ultimately achieve as a coach, but he was far from mediocre. He described himself as "a useful and studious inside right". That was one of his few concessions to self-deprecation. In fact he was a much more accomplished goal-maker and goal-scorer than many of Britain's football historians have acknowledged. Not only that, he had the technique of a juggler.

Shortly before his eighteenth birthday he defied his father, who even then still fostered hopes that he would enter the priesthood, and signed as a semi-professional for the

Lancashire Combination club of his birthplace, Nelson, who later became members of the Third Division (North). A curious footnote in Nelson's records show that several years further on, in 1923, they beat Real Madrid 4-2 in a friendly played in Spain, though, of course, the Real of the time were nothing like the Europe-dominating power they later became.

When he went home and confessed to what he had done his father was livid: "He gave me the book, words and music." He was accused of wasting his hard-won education and joining up with "a crowd of blackguards". His father added the shivering threat that he would never speak to him again. The family had always been close and never believed that anything could fracture the bond. In the middle years of his life Hogan would admit that he realised in some ways his father was right to be disapproving of the sort of men with whom he would be making his life. "Professional footballers were not the choicest people in the land," he said. Not only that, many of them finished their careers without the financial means to support themselves and their families. Worse still, their injuries would turn them into semi-invalids and cost them the chance of any further employment.

For two weeks father and son never exchanged a word, and for several months the relationship remained icy. The situation was made even more tense because the owner of the accountancy firm for whom he was still working demanded to know whether he wanted to be a professional footballer or remain with him. He stalled but knew that soon there would be only one answer.

His teenage friends had tried to persuade him that if he waited clubs much bigger than Nelson, perhaps even Aston Villa, Sunderland, Everton or Preston, would make him an offer. They were right to give their opinion that he was too good for local league football, but he was impatient and so far none of the most famous clubs of the time had shown any interest. Nevertheless, he became an instant success with Nelson. On his first appearance he scored the winning goal against Blackburn Rovers Reserves with a shot that he always said was one of the best in his entire career. The chairman of the club immediately offered him the top money of five shillings a week to which, typically, he replied: "That's not much." It was pointed out that he would join only three other players on such "high wages". He said: "That was good enough for me but my pals were angry." They said he was daft. They reckoned he was worth far more and warned him about the dangers of signing on a match-to-match basis, which in those days was common practice. Being left out of the team or getting injured resulted in not being paid. He was not that pessimistic. "My head was in the clouds. I was walking on air. I was a professional footballer, and that, to me, meant everything."

At the end of a moderately successful season, Nelson offered him an increase to ten shillings but again never being shy to ask for what he thought was the proper reward for his ability, he wanted a further two shillings and sixpence to augment the small salary he was still receiving for his office work. His father, now at last won over by his son's resolve, also argued on his behalf, but there was no agreement.

So, not for the last time in a career of many disputes over money (especially when he was with British clubs), he moved on. This time to the newly formed Rochdale where, financially at least, his talent was slightly better rewarded. They made him captain and paid him fifteen shillings a week but soon wondered whether they had made a serious mistake. Because their home pitch was not ready, they played their first four matches away from home and lost them all. Even so he was the only member of the side not to be thrown out.

Rochdale knew life would be a struggle. The town was a rugby stronghold. Interest in football was minimal. Gate receipts failed to cover costs and soon they had to cut the players' wages by half. In September 1902, after only a year at the club, he had another prolonged argument over money and left. He was confident that if the worst came to the worst at least Nelson would be only too pleased to have him back. In the event there was no need to return. One afternoon while working in the accountancy office a Burnley director he recognised walked in. He said he knew of the "young man's" ability and also that he was not happy at Rochdale. Would he be interested in joining Burnley? "In my eagerness I almost embraced him," Hogan said. "After that it was only a matter of getting my transfer form in order and then I was in my seventh heaven." Burnley were a Second Division club but huge by the standards of Nelson and Rochdale. It was an opportunity he had never dared hope would come…no more accountancy and a decent living wage.

In spite of his initial delight, apart from an increase in salary to £2 a week, his prospects were not exactly rosy. After having been bottom of the Second Division in 1902-03, Burnley had managed to get re-elected but only by a narrow margin and the players had their wages reduced. His own contribution in his first few games was less than memorable. Suddenly he had to play in front of crowds of more than 30,000, ten times more than anything he had experienced before, and the pressure told on his performances. The club's financial situation meant that they had to rely on a lot of young players. They lost 6-0 to Bristol City and 6-2 to Glossop North End but he kept his place and a Lancashire Cup match against Liverpool secured his playing career.

The trainer had told him that he would be up against a full back called Dunlop, whom, ominously, he described as the best in English football. According to the trainer, Dunlop had an enormously strong right foot but poor left. Hogan was advised to exploit that, which he did, forcing Dunlop to attempt tackles

# PROPHET OR TRAITOR?

with his weaker foot. "The first time I received the ball," he said "was from a high clearance. I tried to deflect it to my partner, but I suddenly felt a gust of wind pass my ear. It was from Mr. Dunlop's boot as he punted the ball three-quarters of the length of the field. This did not deter or frighten me. On many occasions that afternoon I had the satisfaction of beating our friend Dunlop by pretending to go to his strong right side and then veering to his left, so unbalancing him." His concentration so impressed the trainer that he was immediately accepted as a regular member of the first team.

Even when he married the local Dragoon Hotel licensee's daughter, Evelyn Coates, with whom he had been at junior school and whose family, like his own, had come from Ireland looking for work, there was never any doubt that football would always take priority in his life. He claimed that apart from the war years his wife was always by his side. Curiously, though, friends who remembered him, and even relatives, said they rarely saw her with him. Although, undoubtedly, in the most successful years of his coaching career the family travelled around Europe together, later she became one of the game's early "football widows", always in the shadow of a man totally involved in what was then a male preserve.

In spite of the Burnley team's uncertain early season performances, he consolidated his position as their regular inside right and occasionally played inside left. Yet the side continued to perform so poorly that the directors threatened not to put them back on full pay unless they beat Grimsby away in one of the last few games of the season. A victory would result in big receipts from the large crowd guaranteed to attend the next match against Manchester United. The team took an early morning train. Hogan left home in such a hurry that he had no time for breakfast, but the club had just about enough money to give all of the players lunch baskets.

# "THE PARSON"

To the amusement and confusion of the rest of the team, he refused the meal. It was a moment that could easily have swayed him away from his resolve to stay true to his religious beliefs. Suddenly he was aware that, for the rest of his days, his principles were more likely to be ridiculed than respected. His strict Catholic upbringing meant that because the picnic included meat he had to go hungry. The match day happened to be one on which the Church demanded that meat was not permitted. Hungry or not, he scored the winning goal in the last minute and, much to his embarrassment, was kissed by the other players (thus disproving the notion that footballers kissing each other on the pitch is some modern phenomenon).

As a result of the win more than 15,000 people attended the next home game against United. At 1-1 he scored a dazzling goal which had an irony about it since he took advantage of the fact that the United goalkeeper liked to throw the ball out rather than kick. In later years he was always an advocate of the throw because he insisted it was more accurate than the kick. On this occasion, though, he quickly noticed where the goalkeeper liked to lob the ball rather casually, and from one of those he rushed across the field, intercepted and hit a twenty-yard half volley into the net not only winning the game but bringing him and his team-mates back on to full pay.

# 3

# On Your Bike

HIS FOUR SUCCESSFUL YEARS at Burnley defied the much-repeated notion that he was an indifferent player. He appeared in fifty-two games and scored twelve goals. One incident in particular was a pointer to his life-long need to be a perfectionist. Having almost walked through an entire defence, he then shot high over the crossbar. At the end of the game he walked dejectedly into the dressing room and asked the trainer whether he thought the position of his shooting foot had been wrong or if, perhaps, he was not properly balanced on the other. The trainer replied: "Just keep on having a pop at goal lad. If you get one out of ten, then you're doing well." He was disillusioned by the absence of technical help but still sure of his own ability. "So from that day I began to fathom things out for myself," he said. "I coupled this with seeking advice from the truly great players. It was through my constant delving into matters that I became a coach in later life. It seemed the obvious thing, for I had coached myself as a quite young professional. It was not easy."

He immediately promised himself that sooner or later he would coach players properly and tell them more about what they were doing wrong than give them the idea that scoring goals was just a matter of pot-luck. He felt it was a fundamental mistake to allow them to repeat their errors without help coming from the trainer. Somewhat grandly he would often remark: "There is a great deal of science about kicking a ball." He became increasingly annoyed that in training the team often went for days without seeing one. All they did was run round the pitch, sprint and do roadwork. "I knew that you simply must train with the thing you use in a match - the ball," he said, adding that football in England remained of a high standard only because of the large number of naturally talented players. He was more concerned about those who had less talent but could become much better if coached rather than simply trained for fitness. However, realising that his own training was helping his fitness but not improving his ability, he bought a ball and worked with it before and after training. At the same time, he felt the need to be even fitter.

He and his father bought a bicycle and placed it on a wooden stand. On the unstable contraption he would cycle up to 30 miles a day without travelling anywhere. In the end, though, he found that his calf muscles were getting rock solid and not helping his speed on the pitch. The Burnley trainer finally found out about the extra training and attempted to overcome the problem of the tight muscles by ordering him to have hot baths and massage with olive oil. Not only that, he dropped him from the first team for two weeks.

His time at Burnley was complicated by the fact that not everyone at the club believed he had a future in football. One of the directors thought he was doing him a favour by trying to guide him into a much different field. He introduced him to a local businessman, Frank Ness, who had an ironmonger's shop and needed a bookkeeper. Surprisingly, Hogan agreed to take up a part-time position. He said that renewing an interest in the world outside football might give him broader vision and even improve him as a player, but in spite of his new security he thought it time to ask Burnley for more money.

# PROPHET OR TRAITOR?

The club had recently appointed a new manager, Seph Whittaker, who refused to pay him the maximum wage of £4 a week. Whittaker's logic was that Hogan was the only player in the first team who was living at home and had another job, so he had less reason to earn the highest salary. In the meantime, in April 1904, Burnley's former manager, Harry Bradshaw (with whom Hogan had got on well), also the club's trainer Jack Stuttard, and full back Harry Ross, all moved down south to Fulham for whom Bradshaw had become the club's first manager. Ross, who had always admired Hogan's subtle ability, recommended that they persuade him to join them.

Bradshaw had never been a player himself and had begun his career in football as Burnley's secretary. He then became chairman before, in 1896, more or less appointing himself as manager. Three years later he moved to London where he revived Woolwich Arsenal at a time when they faced bankruptcy. In 1903-04 he took them into the first division but only after insisting that the team played a short passing game which proved successful enough to save them from oblivion and send them on their way to becoming one of the most famous clubs in the world.

Fulham had been fortunate to get Bradshaw. After all, they were only in the first division of the Southern League, which was the equivalent of today's second division. Successful or not, they had always insisted on avoiding kick and rush but they were not above reproach in standards of morality. Illegal payments to players were rife throughout football and three members of the team were suspended for a year for accepting under-the-counter money.

It was in 1905, at Bradshaw's invitation, that Hogan made his move from the north. Apart from attending boarding school at St.Bede's, it was the first time he had been away from home. On several occasions his mother told one of his sisters, Ellen (ironically, the one who had suggested that a horse and cart would have been preferable to a new brother), to pay unexpected visits to make sure that his digs with an Irish family in Hammersmith were up to scratch and that he was looking after himself. They had no need to worry. He had never been happier: "My football knowledge improved tremendously at Craven Cottage where I found myself amongst the great Scottish players who were playing the style I had been longing for."

His own skill was fundamental to Fulham's winning of two Southern League Championships (1906 and 1907) which gave them the right to join the Football League's Second Division. Bradshaw viewed Hogan's clever but previously under-rated football with enthusiasm yet he offered no help in the way of coaching. The team came to the ground for work-outs, nothing more or less. Even so, to his credit Bradshaw was particularly keen to employ Scottish players who had fine close ball control and always wanted to play a passing game. The easy-going relationship with the playing staff suited his lifestyle, which was shared by most managers of the time. He could leave them to their own devices while he concentrated on office work.

Bradshaw saw his job as organiser of the club and team selector, experimenting continuously. He used sixty-nine different players in five seasons. Hogan thought his style of management badly neglected the need for coaching. On the other hand he agreed with him over the importance of giving the Scottish players their heads since they played in the way he admired. They were the inspiration and touchstone of his coaching career.

In part because of his contribution, Fulham reached the semi-final of the 1908 FA Cup. They beat Luton 9-3 away, Norwich 2-1, also away, then had to go to meet Manchester City with whom they drew before winning 3-1 in a replay at Craven Cottage. By coincidence, in the sixth round they met the other Manchester side, United, and beat them 2-1, but in

# PROPHET OR TRAITOR?

the semi-final they suffered a humiliating 6-0 defeat by Newcastle, whom Hogan considered the finest side he ever faced. He personally was marked out of what was to be his last game for the club by a player often described as the "Prince of Half Backs", Peter McWilliam.

Hogan said the pre-First World War Newcastle side was his favourite since they put emphasis on ingenuity, like a Scottish team. Between 1905 and 1911 they were the outstanding side in the country but were rarely favoured with good fortune. Although they won the League three times in that period, at the same time they reached the Cup Final five times and won the trophy only once. They had the benefit of one of the toughest full-backs of all time in Bill McCracken, who was actually Irish. It was McCracken who more than anyone brought about the historic change in the offside law of 1925. In the years before that, a player was offside unless there were three players, including the goalkeeper, between him and the opposition's goal when the ball was last played. The new law dictated that a player could be offside if only two players were nearer their own goal-line when the ball was last played. Under the old law McCracken and his full-back partner, Frank Hudspeth, had been able to catch opponents offside with monotonous ease.

The seemingly simple change proved to be the most important and controversial alteration in the laws of the game. Until then the centre half had been seen as a potential attacker but the change suddenly meant that defences became much more vulnerable. It was obvious to Arsenal's Herbert Chapman that the centre of the field in a team's own half had to be less of an open gate. In October 1925, in a match against West Ham, he placed Jack Butler in the middle of the defence between the full-backs. Arsenal won comfortably, 4-0. Later Herbie Roberts took over the position with such success that the "stopper" centre half was born. Hogan never much liked the idea, believing it to be a negative move, but in later years had to work with it.

His idea of an entertaining and "correct" side was epitomised in that Newcastle team who lost the 1908 Cup Final 3-1 to Wolverhampton Wanderers. He was amazed at the result - and so were most other people. Wolves were not even challenging for promotion from the Second Division but outplayed Newcastle. All sorts of reasons were put forward, including the length of the grass at Crystal Palace, but it was the third time in four years that the fine team from the north-east had lost in the Final. Not only that, in that same year they were desperate for success because in the first round in the previous season they had lost to a Southern League side - oddly enough, Crystal Palace.

Being at Craven Cottage was a particularly significant experience. It was there that Hogan suffered a serious knee injury that would later cause his premature retirement from playing and, in middle age, leave him in almost permanent pain. But it was also the place where his belief in the way football should be played was founded. He had anticipated that being amongst players of similar philosophy would be beneficial for him as a player, but it also fixed in his mind the way football, played the Scottish way, could blend individual flair with sound teamwork as well as involve changes of pace. Scotland was the bastion of artistic football founded on accurate passing. It was a place where small players with natural ability were the kings and encouraged. He felt comfortable amongst them.

His particular champion was Billy Goldie, a half back who guided him through matches and could not get rid of him afterwards. He would often visit Goldie's house, usually without invitation. Goldie was forgiving and spent hours talking football and giving his advice. Although a considerable talent, he was never capped for Scotland, which amazed Hogan who called the former miner a "football genius". Years later he invited Goldie to see Celtic when he was coaching there and proudly remarked: "We showed him the type of football he had taught me in the old days."

In his four years at Fulham his wide interest in other sports expanded. He was a tennis player of county standard and after taking lessons he had the makings of becoming a formidable boxer. His closest pal was Joe Kenny who had been a professional fighter and was still appearing at exhibition bouts. One evening they met and went to the King's Hall, Hammersmith where Kenny invited him into the ring to take him on. Hogan showed such a natural talent for the sport that he almost knocked him out. It was the first and last time he boxed in public. The following day Bradshaw called him into his office and told him that boxing and football did not and, in the future, would not mix.

Even without any further attempts at boxing, he suffered more than his share of injuries. When he further damaged a knee in training expert help was not available at the club. Because medical standards were poor he carried on playing with only a massage as treatment. If anyone had offered a proper diagnosis it would have been discovered that he had a damaged cartilage. Eventually he was taken to see a surgeon, Herbert Barker, who was later knighted for his medical work in the First World War. Hogan had been unable to play for ten weeks. Barker examined the knee and asked him whether he would like to turn out on the following Saturday.

He thought it was a cruel joke but was given gas and remembered nothing more until he came round, seemingly no longer in pain.. He walked out of the room and into Hyde Park. He tried running: still no pain. He paid three more visits for what today would be called physiotherapy and was declared completely fit. In reality, the knee problem was not cured but given some release. The pain returned and, understandably,

# ON YOUR BIKE

Bradshaw was concerned that the injury would bring Hogan's career to an end sooner rather than later. Hogan himself had also lost some confidence in his own ability to make a full recovery and at the end of the season the manager decided not to retain him, saying that if he broke down the club could not afford to see out the financial terms of his contract (£4 per week). This also meant that Hogan lost the chance of a benefit match (he never had one in his whole career and once remarked, "Sometimes I didn't even get the benefit of the doubt").

After only four appearances in the Second Division, he had no choice but to return to Burnley with whom he was still registered as a Football League player. Realising that word would have spread that he had a suspect knee, he set about making himself as fit as he could by swimming in the sea at Blackpool and training with a friend who was encouraged to tackle him as hard as he liked. Yet the whole experience of seeing his career as a player coming under threat made him think more seriously about a long-term future in coaching. For the time being, though, he was young enough to believe that he was still physically able and skillful enough to continue his career as a player in one of the more minor leagues.

After approaching several clubs he was finally offered a place at Swindon Town, who were then in the Southern League but already had the best inside right in the country, Harold Fleming. In a pre-season trial match Fleming played for the "Probables" while Hogan appeared for the "Possibles". Fleming failed to score a goal. Hogan got three.

To the surprise and annoyance of the fans, in order to accommodate Hogan, Fleming was switched to centre forward. Yet the partnership worked. In his first match Hogan scored four goals against Norwich City to whom, ironically, he had written asking for work and not received a reply. When he scored his fourth goal, Punch Evans (later to be trainer at

41

# PROPHET OR TRAITOR?

Arsenal), who had received his letter, said: "Well I'll be buggered...I could have had you for nothing." Hogan replied: "You should answer your mail." In the same game Fleming added three goals. On the following Wednesday Hogan scored three more against New Brompton (now called Gillingham). He was convinced that bigger clubs would renew their interest, but for the fourth game he was dropped.

Typically, he went straight to the manager who referred him to the directors. They told him that Fleming was a great inside right and was unhappy at being moved to centre forward. He immediately pointed out that far from being deprived, Fleming was still scoring goals. The board, perhaps having in mind that Fleming had become a strong voice in the new players' union, refused to change their mind so Hogan asked for a transfer, which was granted but on the understanding that he played twice more. After the second game, which was against Brentford, he asked to stay overnight with the family with whom he had lodged when he first moved to London. This was refused on the basis that several clubs were interested in obtaining him and he needed to be in Swindon in case forms had to be signed urgently. In fact nothing happened until the following day.

# 4

# A Stranger in Church

ON THE SUNDAY EVENING, as usual, he went to church. In the middle of the service he felt a tap on his back. He looked round. A stranger whispered that he would like to speak to him and that there was another gentleman outside. Hogan said they would both have to wait until after the service was over but he had already begun to wonder whether they were representatives of clubs wanting to persuade him to join. No doubt he hoped and even prayed that they would be from the most famous ones of the time. His mind roamed over the names: Aston Villa, Newcastle, Sunderland. Once the service was over the men introduced themselves as Mr. Tate and Mr. Graves and they were representing Bolton Wanderers. He was far from impressed. Bolton had dropped into the second division and had lost several of their better players. On the brighter side, if he accepted at least he would be going back home to Lancashire.

In spite of his initial disappointment he decided there and then to put his name to an agreement. Mr. Tate remarked: "You know Mr. Hogan, I've signed players at home in bed, under a street lamp and in pubs but this is the first time I've signed anyone at church. Still, it's a good sign lad. I'm not of your faith, but I like to see it." The directors suggested that he went back to the north to find somewhere to live. As further incentive they gave him a railway season ticket from Burnley to Bolton so that he could live in his old home town and train with his new club.

So in October of the season 1908-09, by which time Bolton had played ten League games, he returned to familiar ground. Because of a clause in an earlier agreement with Fulham, Bolton had to pay a total of £600 in fees. Bearing in mind the fact that the transfer record of the time still stood at only £1,000, which Middlesbrough had paid to Sunderland three years earlier to obtain Alf Common and was considered an outrageous amount, the size of the fee suggested that even having had a career-threatening injury he was a considerably better and more valuable player than has sometimes been suggested. He made his debut on November 14, 1908 against Chesterfield. Bolton won 2-0 to set them on their way to a successful season in which he scored fifteen goals. The proof of his ability came in the next when he won a Second Division Championship medal and scored sixteen of the club's fifty-nine goals.

He never spoke much about his regrets, but there is little doubt that if he had ever been asked to choose whether he would rather have been recognised as a highly skilled player than great teacher he would have opted for player. And that was why in all of his coaching he had to prove to his pupils that he had rare skills. He would have loved to be an international and, because of an administrative error, he almost succeeded. His performances at Bolton came to the attention of the Irish Football Association. Their Secretary went as far as to send him a telegram asking whether he would be available to play against England and asked him to confirm that he was born in Ireland. He was so keen to win an international cap that he wired back saying that he was "available", without confirming one way or the other where exactly he had been born.

The Secretary had a few doubts and asked him to provide a birth certificate while at the same time getting in touch with the

Secretary of the English Football Association, Frederick Wall, who discovered that Hogan was born in Nelson. Hogan explained it away with the remark: "When it became known that I had been born in Nelson it was clear there had been some mistake, and that was that." Nevertheless, he later admitted that being deprived of the chance to play at international level was something he rued for the rest of his life. It was a moment in which his usual total honesty was challenged by a desperate desire to be placed amongst the finest players of his day.

The early years of the 20th century saw several of the leading British clubs spend some of the close season on tour abroad. His own first visit, a fourteen-day trip in 1909, took him to Dordrecht, in Holland. Significantly, he loved every minute of his initial taste of a foreign country, not least because Bolton played half a dozen games and never scored less than six goals. Dordrecht themselves borrowed the Dutch national team's goalkeeper, but Bolton still scored ten. His own memory of that game proved that if today we think of claustrophobic man-to-man marking as something comparatively modern, it was around even then. He recalled that Bolton's McEwan was particularly dangerous. The Dutch had heard about him and told one of their players to follow him wherever he went. McEwan got so tired of his shadow that at one point he deliberately ran the ball over the goal-line and behind the goal. The Dutch marker followed him shouting "not allowed." McEwan snapped back: "If it's not allowed (aloud) we'll do it quietly." He lifted the net and kicked the ball into the goal. Quaint though the story now seems, Hogan would later reminisce about the match itself. It persuaded him that one day he would like to "go back and teach those fellows how to play properly".

On returning to real work in the League the following season, he found himself playing for a struggling Bolton. At the end of it they were relegated, along with Chelsea. All of the players had their wages cut, which in those days was a popular way of reducing costs. His own contract had been changed so that he would receive the maximum wage of £4 a week only if he was in the first team. Yet again there was a disagreement and he refused to re-sign. He ended his time with Bolton in 1910 having made thirty-eight first division appearances.

In the early part of the 20th century, when he was in his prime as a player, Continental football had already begun to seek ways of challenging Britain's superiority but it lacked the knowledge to put it under any serious threat. Unofficial England and Football Association representative teams went into Europe and inflicted defeats that often ran into double figures. Yet the development of a skillful style of play soon allowed the Wiener Sportclub of Austria to field a side strong and tactically-educated enough to beat the visiting Sunderland team (who were then third in the Football League) 2-1. Thanks to Hugo Meisl, who first met Hogan when Meisl was playing as an inside forward for FK Austria and later linked with him to form one of the most important manager-trainer partnerships of all time, Austria became a stronghold in the foundation of the game on the Continent.

When the steady erosion of British football's previously unquestioned hold on the game did begin it was in part of its own making. British businessmen working abroad started the very football clubs that years later would not only become some of the most successful and famous in the world, but regularly produced teams that beat the best Britain could offer. The Danes were particularly keen, accepting coaching help from British players and reaching the final of the Olympic Games of 1908 in London where European sides were first seen to be taking the game seriously. Admittedly, Denmark were beaten, almost inevitably by Great Britain, but their football was both effective and attractive. Four years later they again reached the Olympic final and again met Britain whose superior attack was decisive.

# A STRANGER IN CHURCH

Increasingly Hogan was becoming aware that "training" in Britain was failing to improve the natural abilities of the players who at the time were good enough to maintain the required domestic standards of the day but as far as ball control was concerned were not encouraged to improve. Training was almost entirely based on obtaining an acceptable level of physical fitness. Players appearing for the country's leading teams were required to report to the ground by 10am. They would spend an hour or an hour and a half running and skipping and occasionally have a practice match.

A schedule for the Tottenham Hotspur side of 1904 shows that they only came into contact with a football in two sessions in a whole week. They were invited to take a stroll in the afternoon but their coach pointed out that "there is no organised walk". If the next match was particularly important they would be taken away to the seaside or the country for "special training". Some of them realised that their instruction should have been a lot better. One England international of the day wrote an anonymous article in which he confessed that there was "no practice in dribbling, feinting, passing with the inside or the outside of the foot, trapping or heading the ball and placing it with the head like you do with your feet". They rarely saw the manager, who acted more as a secretary and chief executive, while what coaching there was remained in the charge of a trainer who was usually an ex-player from the same club who did little more than bark at them for not running fast enough and carry out some rudimentary massage on injuries.

Among the clubs to do something about the situation was Aston Villa, for whom Hogan later became manager. In 1904 the directors insisted that their staff should spend more time with the ball. One of the outstanding players of the day, J.T. Robertson, said that when he was with Southampton and Everton "all the training we got was light sprinting exercises every Tuesday and Thursday". But he was all in favour of the old system and was one of many who went on record with the sentiment: "A player who has not seen a ball from one match to the other will be keener on the ball than one who has indulged in practice games in the interval." The theory was widespread and lived on for decades, but not on the Continent. Even the esteemed Welsh international winger Billy Meredith was against both training with a ball and the employment of full-time professionals. He said: "If you are living the life you should lead you can put in all the necessary training in spare time and you will play all the better on Saturday for the fact that you have not lived on the ground all the week. Football is like everything else in that you can have too much of it." His rationale was all very well for players with exceptional ability but it did little to improve those who lacked his special talent.

The matches themselves were largely dominated by stout tackling, the bruising shoulder charge and powerful heading. Yet wing half backs and light inside forwards who could also dribble were popular with the crowds, provided that they were fast and not too selfish. Holding up play in the middle of the pitch was not popular. The Scots showed that the best and most effective way to attack was to move the ball swiftly and accurately from defence, through the middle of the field to the forwards. At the same time, though, many of the attackers lacked confidence in their first touch (some things never seem to change) and relied almost entirely on strength. Slowly the majority of clubs moved away from an obsession with physical training, but no British coach put as much emphasis on ball control as Hogan whose recurring knee injury finally ended his playing career.

Across the whole of the Continent football was already being guided by a large outpouring of part-time British player-coaches who had discovered that they were appreciated, and better paid, on the European mainland than at home. In Europe the coach, or trainer as he would have been known, was recognised as being essential, not a luxury of dubious value. Back in England it was commonly assumed that youngsters needed almost no guidance because they could either play well or could not, according to their natural aptitude. So established players spent their summer months teaching where they had pupils who would listen - the "Continentals", as people in Britain would patronisingly describe them. Some of the British players who were near or had reached the end of their careers began to take up full-time appointments either as coaches or officials.

As far back as the opening of the last century John Madden, who had been Celtic's goalkeeper and played for Scotland, was to be found coaching in Prague, where he stayed until he was in his sixties. In 1900 M.D. Nicholson, a former member of the West Bromwich Albion side that won the FA Cup in 1892, was appointed the first president of the Austrian Football Association while at the same time working for the Thomas Cook travel agency in Vienna. It was not uncommon for British companies with foreign offices or factories to advertise at home for workers who also had football experience. Playing football locally created contacts. It was good for business.

The most famous British player to go abroad to coach was Steve Bloomer, the scorer of 352 League goals before he moved to Germany where, like Hogan, he was interned throughout World War I. Gradually, though, the Continent was creating its own talented coaches. Some, including Pozzo, who masterminded two of Italy's World Cup winning teams (1934 and 1938), had spent time in Britain studying and admiring the powerful club sides of the pre-First World War days, not least Manchester United. When acting as technical director of the Italian Olympic side at the 1912 Games, Pozzo first came in contact with Meisl, who was to become the "Father" of the game in Austria and was often called the "Herbert Chapman of European football". Pozzo, Meisl and Chapman were the dominant figures in football between the wars and Meisl became not only Hogan's coaching partner and important influence over his life but his closest friend.

In spite of Hogan's concern about the quality of British football it was still envied and copied. As a result its authorities regarded this as sufficient proof that the game at home could live in unchallenged isolation. Many of the Continental countries had already thought otherwise and in 1904 Belgium, Denmark, France, Spain, Sweden, Switzerland and the Netherlands formed an international federation (FIFA) with which the Football Association in England had a long on-off relationship. Indeed, in the previous year the Union des Societes Francaises de Sports Athletiques had written to the FA suggesting they assisted in the formation of an international governing body. Frederick Wall snootily replied: "The Council of the (British) Football Associations cannot see the advantages of such a federation but, on all matters upon which joint action was desirable, they would be prepared to confer."

British football's aloofness was compounded by the absence of any of the Home Nations from the first three World Cup competitions. Hardly any wonder that Hogan, though passionately devoted to his homeland, always felt professionally vindicated in helping to develop the football of those very Continental countries that in post-Second World War years were to force England to realise by what distance they had been left behind. If the most inward-looking of the English administrators thought him a traitor, it was their own intractable belief that the home of the game in its regulated form had the inalienable right to remain its dominant force both on and off the field that justified his decision to work on behalf of the opposition.

In the earliest years of FIFA's existence it was perhaps understandable that the FA still felt secure. After all on their first official European tour, in 1908, England beat Austria 6-1 and two days later 11-1, Hungary 7-0 and Bohemia 4-0. What the FA chose to ignore was the fact that as each season went by the trickle of players that had been going abroad to coach in order to add to their miserable income had swollen to a substantial river of talent. Robertson, who between 1905 and 1910 was a member of an outstanding Celtic team, assisted Rapid Vienna before becoming part-time coach to MTK Budapest, the club Hogan inspired to become the foundation upon which Hungarian football prospered.

# 5

# A Vow Fulfilled

DURING HIS TIME AT BOLTON Hogan had extended his interest in coaching and was all the time thinking that the British system, with its cynical attitude towards anything progressive, was seriously insufficient. At about the same time that he fell out with the club, he fell in with James Howcroft, an engineer from Redcar who was also Britain's leading referee. Howcroft was fascinated by the progress of the Continental clubs. He often officiated abroad and made a lot of friends amongst the administrators there. He mentioned that he had heard that the very club Hogan had played against on his first visit to the Continent, Dordrecht in Holland, was interested in obtaining a British coach. Hogan had thoroughly enjoyed his short time there as a player and, remembering his vow to go back and teach them more about real, competitive football, he immediately wrote offering his services.

The fact that he had never coached in his life seemed no deterrent to his certainty that he could do the job. He was accepted and in 1910 became the youngest ever British coach to work on the Continent. He was still only twenty-eight: "I was young and foolish to think of going abroad but the urge came over me to teach these foreign lads the proper game."

Looking into the future, it was entirely appropriate that he should start his coaching in the country that many years later, in the golden era of Cruyff, would so impress the world with some of the most versatile football ever seen. The style and tactics of the superb Ajax side that won the European Cup in 1971, 1972 and 1973 was based on the idea that there was no need to hold players to limited responsibilities: defenders could attack and attackers could defend according to the needs of particular situations. But that was a concept Hogan himself knew all about long before the term "Total Football" came into the coaching vocabulary. Versatility was a fundamental part of what he taught. Simply, he expected all of his players except the goalkeeper to be able to change positions and, in the modern phrase, be "comfortable on the ball".

Because he was still technically on the books of Bolton he could only accept a two-season commitment at Dordrecht, who had previously employed several British coaches but always on a casual basis. He quickly discovered that the Dutch players, who mainly came from the universities and were amateurs, had a light-hearted attitude to the game. Although throughout his life he was a pipe and cigar smoker and often had a hip flask tucked under his jacket, he was disgusted by the excessive drinking and smoking habits of the local players. "They drank like fishes and smoked like factory chimneys but they were a jolly lot of fellows, intelligent and able to pick up the science of the game." They listened to him and, in the end, took his advice, sometimes more literally than he expected.

On one occasion he asked the club's centre half to make sure that he never left the side of the opposing centre forward. "At half-time we were leading 1-0, so I went into the dressing room to give my instructions and could not find our centre half, who had played exactly as I asked. I went into the buffet and found him having a beer and enjoying a smoke with the player I had told him to mark. I told him off but had to laugh."

At the same time as coaching Dordrecht, he was asked to prepare the Dutch national side for an away match with Germany. In spite of calling Dutch football of the time

# PROPHET OR TRAITOR?

"primitive", his immediate problem was that the team had two talented inside rights. The selectors insisted that he should play both. His only option was to ask one of them to appear at outside left, a position he was struggling so much to fill that he would have been happy to find anyone of a reasonable standard. He was given two weeks in which to sort out the problem. The main trouble was that both players were very right footed. It was made clear to him that not only did he have to solve the dilemma but that if the team failed, he, not the selectors, would be the one to take the blame. Not surprisingly he was always against selection by committee, which dogged English football until the mid-fifties but was largely abandoned on the Continent much earlier.

In a tough, close game the score was 1-1 with ten minutes remaining. The outside left with no left foot to speak of ("It was just a swinger", Hogan wrote in his diary) had been little more than a spectator for most of the game but suddenly found the ball coming towards him. He automatically volleyed it with his right foot and it hurtled into the net to give Holland victory. The selectors overwhelmed Hogan with their praise, and though he later claimed to have blushed with embarrassment, no doubt he loved every moment of it.

He had gone to his first post in Holland without any pre-conceived ideas about what would be expected of him. At first, much of the coaching he did was basically similar to that done back in Britain except that he placed much greater emphasis on ball control and accurate passing. He always maintained that while short passing with the ball being played thoughtfully from the back was the best and safest option, there was nothing wrong with the accurate long one. He emphasised the word "accurate". The hopeful long ball, which always gives an advantage to the opponents who are facing it when it arrives, was never included in his tactics but the considered one was welcomed. It remains a positive weapon in any team's tactics but in recent years any form of long ball has been branded as an insult to the game's higher ideals. The fact that a modern player as exceptional as Zinedine Zidane, of Real Madrid, often drops deep and plays precise long balls that lead to goals is conveniently ignored.

The Dordrecht players responded well, demanding that he taught them more about mastery of the ball. They were the first foreign pupils to be captivated by his own ball control. He delighted in telling them to kick or throw it at him as hard as they liked and at any height. He would rarely fail to bring it under control. Ironically, it took the arrival of substantial numbers of foreign players into the English Premiership in the 1990s to make everyone aware that one of the basic differences between them and the majority of British-born ones was that they could trap the ball whatever its pace or height. As a result they could pass it with an almost unforgiving velocity rarely previously seen in domestic football.

Early in the 20th century the accepted theory was (and in Britain it remained for many more years) that above all considerations for skill, the players who were the fittest would almost invariably finish matches the stronger and so have the greater chance of winning. Once abroad Hogan never altogether forgot that essential but he quickly invented routines to create fitness that almost always involved the ball. The football he demanded was what he called "the old Scottish game". He described it as "an intelligent, constructive and progressive, on-the-carpet manner". All of the players who came into contact with him recalled the description "on the carpet manner", which became his theme phrase.

There was another essential difference between football back in Britain and the game on the Continent, and it had little to do with tactics. British football had been established in the working class, with the growth of professionalism offering a few young men an opportunity to raise themselves out of

# PROPHET OR TRAITOR?

poverty. In Europe football was still little more than an enjoyable pastime attracting youths and men from a range of backgrounds. At the beginning few of them thought of becoming professionals yet they had a relentless hunger to improve their skills.

Near the end of his long life he looked back at those early days in his coaching career and said: "I was astonished to find the class of men playing football when I first arrived in Holland. And I quickly realised that with such intelligent people it was of no use my giving orders to go out for a kickabout or a sprint. I simply went on the field and worked with them. Then it was a case of thinking out little ideas and exercises in shooting, ball control, trapping, heading, combination stunts, and afterwards playing in side games with them: all manner of men from the working man's son to the son of a millionaire. Then followed work in the class-room with the aid of a blackboard and copy books; the thousands of questions and answers."

Although he enjoyed his work with the promising Dutch, in his heart he was still a frustrated player. He was convinced that he had at least another season left in him. So he returned to Bolton where the club had a particularly skillful left-side partnership formed by Ted Vizard and Joe Smith. Hogan was so impressed he said it was as if they had telepathic communication. Many years later a few England managers, notably Don Revie, realised that it could (though there was no guarantee) greatly ease early problems in charge of a national team if instead of looking for the eleven best players in the land, the manager searched for as many as were available who played for the country's most successful club. Hogan always remembered that partnerships could be valuable in building effective teams. Bolton were promoted to the First Division but his future was not with them, but in coaching.

56

# A VOW FULFILLED

If partnerships are important amongst players, equally they can be the links that make some managers and coaches become powerful companions. While never slow to draw attention to his own ability, nevertheless Hogan was not reluctant to mention that his career on the Continent was guided, prompted and supported by Meisl whom he described as "the greatest man I ever met in football", adding, "I had great respect for Herbert Chapman, but I never met a football man like Meisl. He knew the football style and technique of every footballing country." Sometimes working in tandem and occasionally simply corresponding, they generated the remarkable Austrian "Wunderteam" of the 1930s.

Their first partnership, formed in the English close-season of 1912, was based on Meisl's life-long pessimism. Austria had been involved in a tough international match with Hungary, which was refereed by Howcroft. Afterwards Meisl, who was what we today might call the "supremo" of Austrian football, was worried about the consequences and asked Howcroft to give his opinion of the way his team had played. Howcroft said he felt they needed a "trainer" who would bring out the best of their under-developed skills. He suggested Hogan whom Meisl immediately invited for six weeks to coach the national squad, which was preparing for the Olympic Games in Stockholm, and several club teams.

Initially Hogan failed to impress the Austrians. They found it difficult to understand him while his coaching seemed too concerned with basic principles. They had expected to be taught winning football overnight. Meisl spent an evening talking to him about the particular requirements of coaching on the Continent. Hogan's mind raced ahead. He began to realise that between them they could shape a style of football which was based on the concept of letting the ball do most of the running and the players taking advantage of open space. The fact that few of the players he had seen could shoot to save their lives seemed unimportant. As for tactical formations, neither he nor Meisl felt it essential to be too rigid. At the time they remained convinced that the centre half should play an important role in what today is called "midfield" and that the five forwards should play more or less in a line.

He soon found that the Austrians were so keen to play technically correct possession football that they never risked using the long ball. He had to reiterate what he had said so often in his earlier days in Holland: that the long ball was a legitimate and useful way of opening up a defence, provided it was played carefully and to players with sufficiently good skills to bring it under control. Further evidence of that could be seen from the great Hungarian side of the 1950s who employed it well but sparingly.

In spite of his inexperience, he soon had his Olympic side making substantial improvements. The players warmed to his personal enthusiasm and, in practice matches, it was a winning hand that he could take the place of any of them in any position and play equally as well, if not better. They took on a touring Tottenham Hotspur team and won 1-0, then drew with Southampton, a club in the forefront of touring and always willing to put on a show. The Saints goalkeeper was Jack Robinson, a former England international who before matches would put on demonstrations of his dexterity. Obviously the Southampton players hardly made it difficult for him and he performed spectacular saves from comparatively easy shots but the Austrians were so impressed that from then on they called any especially-good stop a "Robinsonsave".

The committee members of the Austrian FA were suitably won over by the improvements in their national team and, shortly before the party travelled to Sweden, they organised a farewell banquet at which Hogan was the principal guest. It was the least they could do since they never had the money to

A VOW FULFILLED

pay him a respectable wage and he had to depend on financial assistance from the clubs he had also coached.

In Stockholm, he tried to remain patriotic. He made it obvious that he greatly enjoyed seeing the Great Britain side perform outstandingly well to beat Denmark 4-2 before his own Austrian team overcame the Germans 5-1. Subsequently Austria were knocked out 4-3 by the Dutch. So they went into a "Consolation Final" which they lost to Hungary. He took the outcome sorely. He said he thought Austria were better than Holland "who had the benefit of my coaching in the years before I started my work in Austria" - a bitter and immodest comment, but not without an element of truth. Significantly, he also expressed a lot of interest in Italy who, he said, had been "hopelessly outclassed" but, he thought, could become a meaningful power in world football. It was a portentous remark. Under the guidance of Pozzo, that is exactly what they became.

In one of many indications of his being years ahead of the times, Hogan studied controlled diets (which in England have only been taken seriously since the arrival in the 1990s of several Continental coaches). He said that the amount of meat the Austrian Olympic players were eating when he took over their training "scared me". He insisted on more green vegetables and at every meal stewed fruit was always available. In contemporary terms it was rather like Arsène Wenger's experience of weaning the British players at Arsenal off a regular intake of steak and chips (or anything else with chips) and on to more pasta and chicken, not to speak of questioning the wisdom of over-indulgence in alcohol.

The time had come to reflect on his playing career. One match in his final season (1912-13) as a player remained in his memory for the rest of his days. It was at Middlesbrough. A close relative of a gale was blowing straight down the field and in the first half Bolton were facing it. Among the players on the

59

other side was one of the most famous in British football's history, Steve Bloomer, a centre forward of exceptional goalscoring gifts (as well as his 352 League goals he scored twenty-eight in twenty-three matches for England). Against Bloomer for Bolton was the rather more physical Sammy Greenhaigh. They hammered each other without mercy until, somewhat foolishly, Greenhaigh told Bloomer that he would never score against him. Shortly before half-time Middlesbrough were awarded a penalty. Bloomer picked up the ball, placed it on the spot, turned to Greenhaigh and said: "What were you saying?" He slammed the ball in to win. Hogan would often talk about the incident but something he considered much more important stuck in the memory.

The one thing he never forgot was not so much Bloomer's wit as the importance of something seemingly as trivial as the toss. Bolton had elected to play against the wind. In the end they ran out of energy and though he was all against believing that fitness was everything, he was realistic enough to accept that an exhausted side had little chance of performing well in the final stages. He also noted that the position of the sun in the first half was important. He was always careful to demand that if it was to set low behind one of the goals, his captain, if he won the toss, would make sure the opponents had that problem in the second half. His attention to detail was to be essential in his rise to become one of the most successful "trainers" of players in Europe. He encouraged every team he coached to take advantage of the natural elements.

# 6

# Meisl Trumps the Spy

AFTER THE 1912 OLYMPICS and his return to Britain to clear up his affairs with Bolton, he was determined to go back to the Continent and pick up his new career. In the following year he spotted an advertisement from the German FA inviting applications by British coaches. He responded and was asked to attend an interview at the Adelphi Hotel in Liverpool. There he was surprised to find more than twenty other applicants, almost all of them well-known players who had done some coaching. "I almost gave up the ghost then and there," he said. He was the last to be interviewed by a German schoolteacher who was working in the city. He later heard that soon after the First World War began his interviewer disappeared, having spent a lot of his time in Britain spying for Germany.

He was asked if he spoke German. He said he did, without actually revealing the considerable limitations in his vocabulary. To his amazement he was told that he had every chance of getting the job and it would soon be confirmed in writing. In the event, the German FA all too innocently contacted Europe's most knowledgeable expert on coaching and coaches, Meisl in Austria, to ask for as much information as he had about Hogan's ability and character. The move backfired. Meisl immediately contacted Hogan and offered him alternative employment - to coach the Austrian International XI for the proposed Olympic Games of 1916.

# PROPHET OR TRAITOR?

Bloomer, whom Hogan always thought was a truly world class player, was given the job in Germany.

Hogan's work with the Austrian FA quickly expanded and in spite of all the warnings that the First World War was not far off, he decided to arrange for his wife and two children to join him in Vienna. No doubt by then Evelyn had been married to him for long enough to realise that she would always have to share her husband with football and that football would always demand much the greater part of his time. She and the children would go with him all over Europe yet she had virtually no interest in the game, which of course in those days was nothing unusual amongst women.

Even before the 1920s he had been predicting that sooner or later the Continent would catch and overtake British football. He pointed out that England had been "world beaters" in several other sports, including tennis, but had been left behind by countries in which serious coaching had raised standards. He was particularly aware that Continental rugby was making significant progress. He said that if it was time for British football to wake up, similarly it was time for Britain to realise that in many of those other fields they were about to be turned into also-rans. Meisl and Pozzo were in the forefront of those Continental minds guiding the revolution.

Meisl came from a wealthy Jewish family in Vienna and, naturally, his father steered him towards a business career. However, his son was devoted to football and played with moderate success for the local British-formed Cricketers Club. In an attempt to divert his son's attention back to what he considered more important matters, his father sent him off to Trieste to do office work. There he became fluent in Italian but at the same time he studied several other languages, particularly English, which he perfected. He had a great love of England and its football, which was fortunate for Hogan.

# MEISL TRUMPS THE SPY

During his time in Italy Meisl had kept in close touch with Johann Leute, who was one of Austria's leading players at the time. As a result he continued to be well informed about what was going on back in his home country. He was called back to Austria to complete military service after which his father tried to talk him into going into banking, this time with a degree of success. He did the job, though reluctantly, and at the same time began working for the Austrian Football Association.

Meisl's administration work for the Austrian FA became ever more time consuming and successful. Most of it was to do with the raising of funds, but he dearly wanted to play a more practical role in the development of his country's football talent. After all, he had seen how Hungary had been making impressive progress. He welcomed the opportunity to work with and advise Hogan, whose theories on football and how it should be played were much the same as his own - they had both been ball-playing inside forwards who deplored kick and rush and the speculative long-ball game.

Hogan was suddenly in a dream world. In spite of his love of his home country and county, he could not resist saying: "This was a revelation to me. To leave my dark, gloomy industrial Lancashire for Gay Vienna was just like stepping into paradise. The Emperor Francis Joseph was on the throne and Vienna, in those days, was really a city of love, life and laughter." His wife and children, Joe and Mary, were equally at home.

He was immediately asked to coach the Olympic team twice a week and for the remainder of the time work with the leading Austrian club sides. He remarked that, in spite of initial problems, his efforts at coaching the Austrians convinced him that he wanted to remain employed full-time on the Continent. He was amazed at the enthusiasm of the local players. In fact he was so busy that he had to arrange for those from Vienna FC to be coached between 5.30 and 7.30 a.m. The idea came from them.

# PROPHET OR TRAITOR?

At his first training session with the Olympic group he acted cautiously. He carried out what would have been a fairly normal morning's work, finishing with a practice game. Afterwards the captain, looking disappointed, approached him and asked whether that was a typical session in England. Hogan again had to accept that the demands of Continental players were going to be much different to those at home. Until then he had been concerned that his determination to revolutionise football training would be too demanding. He wanted to break the players into his ideas as sympathetically as time would allow. Now he realised that they wanted everything he could give, and quickly. He told Meisl about the difficulties and Meisl thought that the main problem had been a lack of communication. He stressed that it would be essential for Hogan to demonstrate everything that he wanted the players to do. It was advice that played into Hogan's hands since that was his special talent.

He worked through many a night planning much more technical sessions, with far more emphasis on ball play. "That was the vital time when I really became a football coach," he said. It was also a time in which he met a number of youngsters who were to lose their lives in the First World War. The extinguishing of so many promising players throughout Europe was immense, and those who did survive forfeited what should have been the best years of their careers.

His coaching at a comparatively early age had one big advantage. His own playing career was not just a faint memory. He had been performing at a high level so recently that he could be fully involved in the coaching sessions. But that was something upon which he insisted even in his seventies. He always said that he would never attempt to teach anything that he himself could not perform (even so, over the years many professionals of high reputation would despair simply because they could not properly reproduce his skills). The Austrians were highly impressed with his mastery of the ball in practice games.

# MEISL TRUMPS THE SPY

Still in his early thirties, nevertheless he was made solely responsible for Wiener Amateur SV (later to become FK Austria Vienna), for whom Meisl had played with fragile skill. The club was one of those based on British roots, having been formed in the 1890s as Vienna Cricket and Football Club by Baron Rothschild's gardeners, James Black and William Beale. Curiously, in view of Hogan's later involvement with Hungarian football, in 1897 the Vienna club had played BTC of Budapest in one of football's earliest friendly matches between teams from different countries

What made him special and different from the other trainers was that he remained true to an immovable principle: no footballer could realistically claim to be worth his place in a team of high standard unless he could instantly control the ball, pass with reliable accuracy, short or long, and understand the value of movement into free space. It was the pass and move principle that became the basis of coaching for many fine teachers, including Arthur Rowe at Tottenham, and Ron Greenwood, the West Ham and England manager who found Hogan's ideas to be stimulating. That principle, which many years later was the foundation of the Hungarian football that finally showed England the limitations of their less sophisticated, more direct way of playing, would be the cornerstone of Hogan's work. In Britain the emphasis on ball winning, heading ability, stamina and power above the values he held with a passion was to become an impediment lasting for decades. Indeed, British football of the 1920s, especially that played so brilliantly by Celtic, Rangers and the Scottish national team, sadly became not the trademark for continuing success at home but the guide for the emerging footballing countries of Europe and South America.

Hogan was not alone in warning that British supremacy would soon be erased if more emphasis was not placed on the very skills that football in Scotland had developed. The

# PROPHET OR TRAITOR?

journalist James Catton was making just such a point in 1923 when he warned that England would lose her prestige unless the players "use more intelligence, and by constant practice obtain control of and power over the ball with the inside and outside of the foot". He said that unless they "got out of the rut into which they have fallen" the game would lose its popularity in Britain and its world-wide fame. In that same year the former England centre forward William Hibbert abandoned his work as a coach in England to teach the game in, of all places, New York. His bitter parting words were: "As they know all about it in this country, there is no room for me here. Our young players prefer not to be taught."

Even in the last few years of the twentieth century, when foreign players and coaches were widely employed in League football, the English national team consistently failed to succeed, less for tactical reasons than because so few of the chosen players had the ability to change the course of a game with individual invention and intervention. The 2002 World Cup finals campaign in which, admittedly, England began promisingly with their victory over one of the favourites, Argentina, nevertheless floundered on an inability to match skill with skill. Not one England player, including the free-kick and passing expert David Beckham, consistently took on and beat more than one opponent or controlled the ball with the seemingly effortless mastery of every single outfield member of the far from special Brazilian squad. Tommy Docherty, who as a youngster at Celtic took on board so many of Hogan's ideas, is fond of saying that the majority of modern British players often "trap the ball as far as I could throw it". No wonder that when, at last, in 2003 a 17-year-old called Wayne Rooney appeared in an England shirt and actually took the ball past a few opponents, he was immediately and absurdly compared with some of the greatest players of all time, even including Pelé. His skill was a refreshing pleasure to see but in reality he was doing no more than dozens of young Continental and South American players achieved as a matter of course.

With the important assistance of Hogan, Austria led the way in questioning the all-powerful hold that British football had enjoyed and presumed it would retain indefinitely. Yet anyone unfamiliar with the power that was once Austrian football might look back to an event as comparatively recent as the early 1990s and ask what befell the country that, some twenty years before the famous Hungarian Magyars of the Fifties, produced a team that came to London and made England look ordinary. In the qualifying competition for the 1992 European Championship, Austria lost 1-0 to the Faroe Islands. It was the national team's lowest point in their long and once illustrious football life and was in complete contrast to the era in which Hogan was their coach.

Austria was one of the first countries in Europe to embrace the idea of improving football standards by taking on regular international matches. Their first had been played as early as 1902 when they beat Hungary 5-0. Apart from some unofficial games, no other international had been played beyond matches between the countries of the United Kingdom. Up until the late 1950s Austria went on to produce highly respected teams, though none as good as those formed in the Hogan-Meisl era between the wars.

Being in Austria perhaps involved as much of a learning process for Hogan as it did for the local players. Everything he believed about the inadequacy of coaching back at home in England was put into full focus. Making physical domination of matches the priority was not the Austrians idea of getting things in the right order. Their players understood that it took no special skill to get fit. They did that automatically. They demanded much more.

When he made an occasional return visit to England he took every opportunity to talk about the Austrians appetite for

# PROPHET OR TRAITOR?

learning about football as he thought it ought to be played - on the ground and with individuality prized. To anyone who would listen he preached a sermon of doom. He insisted that while on the Continent he could work with receptive young players, in England there was nothing but head-in-the-sand indifference to those who were on the verge of turning the world of football on its axis. A lot of people heard him or read what he wrote but few believed what he was saying.

The message was as relevant then as it was years later. How often in the 1950s, '60s and even '70s did we listen to commentators say that the English teams, at club and national level, would inevitably overcome their Continental opponents because "fitness will tell in the end"? But in the end, the "Continentals" became equally fit, a lot more inventive and better at dictating the velocity at which they wanted a game to be played. Even in the 1990s English teams who were obviously struggling to combat more skillful foreign sides were supposed to be encouraged by hearing that "the goalkeeper is suspect on crosses" or that the opposing central defenders were allegedly unhappy against big, powerful centre forwards. If they did seek out and find any of those faults it was poor compensation for being largely outwitted and outmanoeuvred in midfield.

With the Austrian players expecting him to raise their standards of competence, which were already markedly higher than he had experienced when he first played abroad for Bolton, Hogan continued to spend hours, almost always at night, writing more and more training schedules which would reflect his determination to foster the passing game and individuality without losing sight of the better aspects of British football. He never despised the players back home but was saddened because he was convinced that they were led by people who were misguided, or simply too stuck in their ways to see that the game was changing.

# MEISL TRUMPS THE SPY

He had soon recognised that the level of skill amongst large numbers of the Austrians could form the basis of a revolution. At first the language barrier had created problems but the idea of making "friends" with the ball (a term modern coaches seem to believe they invented) was another of his slogans and required little interpretation. His own relationship with a football said more than any amount of lecturing. On several occasions when he felt the players he was coaching needed some extra inspiration, he would place a ball between himself and one of them and walk back some twenty yards. He then asked the player to kick or throw another football at him. He would control it with his first touch and knock it back with the second, hitting the ball placed in the middle not less than eight times out of ten. Whether this did actually inspire or intimidate is hard to say.

His burning of the midnight oil in preparing for his coaching sessions was to lead to what became known as the "Viennese School" of football, which was based on making sure that players who were not in possession always looked for areas in which they could be found with a simple pass; that possession was the essence of victory and that a ball travelling on the ground was much more likely to reach its intended receiver than one lobbed hopefully forward into the grateful possession of the defenders who always had the positional and visual advantage. His life-long obsession with the art of keeping the ball at pitch level was always slightly at odds with his personal delight in showing players how he could even head the ball into submission.

Football in pre-First World War days had not long evolved from a much more disorganised game in which tactical teamwork played little part. In the late 19th century it was commonplace to have matches in which eight forwards would attack the opposition's goal, which would be defended by a goalkeeper and two others. It was when the Scots decided that it was better to move the ball in a more considered way that their tactically thoughtful football began to spread around the world. It had helped when the rules changed to allow the ball to be transported forwards as well as backwards!

Slowly football moved towards the long-lasting formation of five forwards, three half backs and two full backs. After a time some teams decided that the line of five attackers should be altered to allow two of them to act as withdrawn inside forwards, which considerably increased the more subtle qualities of the game. Although an inside forward himself, albeit a front-running, goalscoring one, Hogan was far from convinced by the changing pattern and decided that the Austrian national team would have five forwards, with the inside forwards tending to stay in line with the centre forward rather than dropping behind, and three half backs with the centre half supporting them.

When, in 1925, the offside rule changed, most teams ordered the centre half to become a central defender but Austria continued to insist on the old system. In spite of what might have seemed to be a rigid pattern it still allowed a surprising amount of freedom of expression. Hogan identified the rule change as the single most important reason why England, as he put it, "surrendered our mastery in European football affairs". He pointed out that it became less difficult for a player to get offside "and our clubs went into a real flap and defence became the watchword". Chapman, he pointed out, had the men at Arsenal to carry out the plan. "Other clubs tried to copy him but they had not the men, and the result was, in my opinion, the ruination of British football, with the accent on defence and bringing about the big kicking game which put to an end the playing of constructive football. Through this type of game our players lost the touch and feeling for the ball." He said that while he remained in charge of Austria, his employers sent him back to Britain to study the "new style". When he returned he admitted to them that this was not going to be some short-term tactic, but the Austrians insisted that they wanted to maintain an attacking style. He had been "amazed" that Scottish clubs had taken on the third back game and was relieved when in 1931 his Austrian side beat Scotland 5-0 in Vienna.

Meisl was impressed with Hogan's obstinate determination both at club and international level and was full of hope for a successful 1916 Olympics, but war intervened. Meanwhile, Hogan himself had won such a reputation over the whole country that he could claim that his word on football was "law". He said the "Hogan School of Football" was known throughout the country. His young son Joe began to join him at training sessions. "He was still only three and still in skirts but people marvelled at the way he could kick, head and control a ball. Joe was certainly an example to those people of what a British boy could do with a ball." The idea of a three-year-old heading a leather football would today have many onlookers scurrying off to have the child taken into care.

In spite of the gathering gloom of war, life was pleasant. The family often joined Meisl at dinner or for concerts. Hogan would compare Austrian football with a Viennese waltz ("light and easy"). Suddenly everything changed. He realised that life could be made extremely difficult for the family, so he went to the British Consul in Vienna and asked whether it would be advisable to get back to Britain urgently. "The Consul assured me that there was no immediate danger and advised me to carry on with my work. Within forty-eight hours of that interview war was declared. What a mess we were in to be sure."

# 7

# Prison

AT DAWN ON THE FIRST MORNING of what was to become known as the Great War but which was the most bestial of them all, there was a knock on the door of their flat. His wife answered. It was the police who were searching the city for foreign nationals. Being so well known, he was easily found. They simply walked in and arrested him. With Evelyn and the children in tears, he was physically pulled out of bed and led away to the local police station where he was cross-examined and then interned as a civilian prisoner of war in the Elizabeth Promenade Prison. There he was joined by many other British people who had been working in the country before the outbreak of war or just happened to be in the wrong place at the wrong time. He had not even been allowed to collect up any of his personal possessions, not even a razor.

When, several days later, his wife visited him she said he "had the appearance of a real convict with three days' growth on his chin". For a man always meticulous about his appearance, his stubble distressed him almost as much as the miserable prison cell. He was offered a frightening apology for being held there. The guard told him: "The concentration camps are not ready." He was also informed that the Austrians were only acting on orders from Berlin. There was no chance of appeal, especially as in those days it had been possible to

# PRISON

travel in Europe without a passport. None of the family held one, which greatly added to the problems. In effect they were stateless.

Some years later he related his own version of the experience to the Burnley Express: "I was thrown into prison along with thieves and murderers. My wife and children were frightened to death and had to make a shift for themselves. I eventually got out of this prison, but the Austrian FA broke my contract and left us to starve. Our story of hardship is too long to relate in detail. Suffice it to say that the American Consul sent my wife to England in March, 1915, and I was saved by two Englishmen who had obtained their freedom by giving £1,000 to the Austrian Red Cross." His wife was pregnant with a third child and had appealed to the American Consul for help, which he gave by arranging transport to the French coast. Even so, the journey took eleven days, with the last few miles on board ship becoming a gamble with the German navy's submarines. She went to stay with members of her family in Blackpool but was ill with exhaustion. Son Frank was born a few months after she got back to England but he was not seen by his father until after the War was over, more than three years later.

The Englishmen who "saved" him were actually the Blythe brothers, Ernest and Eddie, who had owned a large departmental store in Vienna and were married to Austrian women. They had quickly gained their parole and, as well as making their substantial contribution to the Red Cross, offered guarantees to the authorities that if released Hogan would be of good behaviour, which was hardly a risk. Only a matter of a few hours before he was due to be moved to a concentration camp, he was allowed to go and went to live with the Blythe family. For two years he acted as their odd job man. As well as the "villains" with whom he had been in prison, there were British doctors, actors, holidaymakers and Baron Rothschild's staff including the butler, footmen, maids and gardeners. All had been caught up in the sudden round of arrests and many were less fortunate, spending the rest of the war behind bars.

He helped teach the Blythe children English and sports, particularly tennis, which he loved and still played to a high standard. He had to report on a regular basis to the police and was always under curfew. The conditions of his release from prison included an undertaking that he would not go near railway stations or important buildings, especially barracks. Meanwhile, he kept himself fit by doing PT exercises in the Blythe's large garden.

Eventually, late in 1916, he was told that he could leave Austria. He had no idea where he would be taken but arrived at the Hungarian border. He was handed over to a guard who spoke some German and told him he was lucky and that he was going "home". His eyes widened. "To England?" "No to Budapest." He snapped back: "Budapest is not my home." To which the guard could only reply: "It will be if you behave yourself." It was clear that for the remainder of the war he would remain an internee, but at least he would be in a country that he felt confident would in the future warm to his coaching and blossom under its guidance.

His arrival in the Hungarian capital was not unnoticed. He was met by a delegation of local sports officials and Baron Dirstay, who had been educated at Cambridge University and was an influential financial supporter and vice-president of the MTK club. The Baron had heard about Hogan being kept prisoner in Austria and had worked with the Hungarian and Austrian authorities to have him brought out. Hogan was told that a job would be made available on the condition that he reported on a regular basis to the police and never discussed the war with anyone. The position was as trainer to MTK whose president, Dr. Arpad Brulls, a famous wrestler in his day, was determined to make the club the most powerful in

Europe, no matter what the cost. Hogan was given his own office at the stadium where the facilities were far superior to anything in Britain or anything he had previously experienced on the Continent.

MTK were already on the road to becoming enduringly successful, winning the Hungarian championship in every season from 1917 to 1925. So he was enormously grateful for the opportunity to become their guide, saying: "I can never forget the kindness of the Hungarians and their hatred of the Germans and Austrians." However, he faced an unpromising situation. His biggest problem was that most of the regular first team players were serving in the Army. Occasionally they would return and be able to play in the odd match but there was no choice other than to create a new team mainly from young players. Among them were Gyorgy Orth, who first appeared for Hungary at the age of 16 and was to play for his national side in five different positions, and Jozsef "Csibi" Braun, a fast and skillful right winger. Hogan discovered them when they were simply kicking a ball about in Budapest's Angol (English) Park. They became two of the finest players ever to appear for Hungary. Another of the promising youngsters he helped to develop was Alfred Schaffer, who became a formidable goalscorer and later moved to Germany where he was to be known as the "Fussballkonig", or "Football King". Several British clubs tried to sign him, including Sunderland and Blackburn Rovers who had played against him on tour, but he refused to go.

Schaffer was never short of confidence and once told the national team's acrobatic goalkeeper, Ferenc Plattko, that he would score six against him when they met in a League match the following weekend, and he did. Hogan took him to one side and told him it was a boast that he should never repeat because it was almost certainly an unrepeatable achievement. In a way that he had not anticipated it was an unnecessary warning.

# PROPHET OR TRAITOR?

Plattko left Vasas to join MTK, who also signed Imre Schlosser from Ferencvaros, whose fans were furious. Schlosser compensated them by scoring fifty-nine goals in seventy-two international matches for Hungary (a record that stood until the time of the Magic Magyars of the 1950s).

Technically, all of the players in the MTK team of the period were supposed to be amateurs but Dr. Brulls subsidised them to such an extent that Schaffer, the biggest of the stars, was paid £2,000 a year for a fictitious job in a Budapest office. It was Meisl, a banker, who when secretary of the Austrian FA after the First World War promoted an early form of open professionalism which spread across Europe. Schaffer took advantage of the new riches available in the game and transferred to Nuremberg. Others also moved on and after their period of domination MTK gradually lost their hold on success and remained sidelined until regaining strength in the Thirties.

Schlosser was one of many players who found Hogan's rigid attitude towards discipline almost too much to take. Whenever he scored a goal he had a harmless but annoying habit of spitting in the back of the net. Hogan's sensitivity was deeply offended. He threatened not to coach Schlosser unless he stopped, which eventually he did but only after many months of persuasion. Other members of the team felt that the issue had been taken out of all proportion but none took Schlosser's side against Hogan.

Even though he was happy to be working in Hungary, Hogan was depressed by the fact that he did not see his family for most of the war. Even when it ended he was troubled by the cost of living. In March 1919 he sent a letter to the Burnley Express saying "I am quite broken down financially. It would open the eyes of some of our people. A suit of clothes cost from £80 to £110, a pair of boots from £12 to £20, and tea costs £9 9s per 1lb, and I have a wife and three little children to support". He was sending most of his income back to them in Britain.

# PRISON

His initial stay with MTK lasted three years (1916, 17 and 18) and in each season the club grew stronger and better than the opposition. The end of the war meant that football was revived and at the same time his reputation began to grow again. He was known as a coach/trainer who could spot and nurture the best of the country's young talent, most of which arrived at the door of MTK who generally supplied the largest proportion of players to the Hungarian national team. His ability to see a youngster playing on a local park and know that there was a spark awaiting the gentle breeze of encouragement was something that not only gave him great satisfaction but led to a host of players owing him their thanks.

His finding of Orth and Braun was an example of his sharp eye for potentially exceptional players. The two youngsters impressed him even without seeing them play in an organised match. He discovered that they were both at school. They had been learning English and were excited to attempt a conversation. He invited them to the MTK club on the basis that he would not only coach them in football but also English. He said he felt like a gold prospector who had found two nuggets. "I pounced on them and said 'they are mine, my very own'."

Orth and Braun went to the club the following day and joined up. Hogan said: "They were both intelligent lads attending High School in Budapest. Every day after school I had them on the field, instructing them in the art of the game. The Hungarians mature very quickly and they quickly moved into the MTK first team." They both made their first appearances for Hungary against Austria in Vienna. Hogan described Orth as "the most versatile, greatest and most intelligent player I have ever seen" and suggested that he was even better than the majestic Johnny Carey, the Manchester United and Ireland international, because he could play in virtually every position. As for Braun, Hogan said he was one of the finest outside rights with whom he ever worked. Most Hungarian football historians would say that he was the best the country has ever produced.

When Meisl, who was still coaching the Austrian national team, first saw Orth and Braun he asked Hogan "Where on earth did you discover those two lads?". He said that he was amazed at their ability and that "they played like well developed English internationals". Hogan considered that to be the highest possible praise from the man he respected more than any other and said that no coach could produce great players unless they had some inborn talent. He would often say: "You can't vaccinate a player with football."

He was thrilled but a shade embarrassed when his former club, Bolton Wanderers, came on tour and a combined Budapest side under his guidance beat them 4-1. He said: "I sat next to Mr. Foweraker, manager of the ex-Cup winners, and he exclaimed 'Marvellous'." In spite of that defeat and his magnanimous praise for the opposition, Charles Foweraker remained manager until 1944 (a total of twenty-five years).

Hogan mulled over his latest chance to compare the Hungarians he was coaching and the players from home. "I only wish that the British player who argued with me a few months ago that swerving and feinting were natural gifts which could not be taught had the opportunity of playing against these two wonders (Orth and Braun). They would very quickly have changed their views on the matter, and after all is said and done, this body control was only learnt by simple exercises, such as dribbling the ball round sticks and controlling it first with the inside and afterwards with the outside of the foot, coupled with gymnastic exercises to make the body loose at the hips. Could you imagine asking a British player to do anything like this? Yet this is what Continental teams - who keep on beating English League XIs - are doing to prepare their players for the battle of football supremacy."

# PRISON

Orth was probably his greatest discovery. While later generations would see Ferenc Puskas, Nandor Hidegkuti, Sandor Kocsis and Jozsef Bozsik form the basis of the "Magic Magyars", there was perhaps even more magic in the MTK side for whom Orth was the undoubted star. Although over six feet tall, he was unusually agile. He was also a fencer of international standard. He had presence, persuasive powers of leadership and occasionally, in an injury crisis, would go in goal, even at international level.

Hogan saw Orth not only as his protege but almost as another son. When in a match against FK Austria in 1925 one of the Austrians, Tandler, ruthlessly ran into Orth's outstretched leg, Hogan immediately knew that the injury was serious. Orth was carried off and lifted into a van. As the doors closed, Hogan, tough in spirit though he was, burst into tears. Although months later Orth made an attempt to play again and appeared in one last international, he was never able to reclaim the form that before his terrible injury had drawn huge crowds to watch his every appearance. With help from Hogan, he took up coaching, eventually moving to South America, then Italy and Portugal. Sadly he was on his way back to Hungary, where he intended to settle for good, when he suffered a fatal heart attack.

Braun, whom Hogan had encouraged to dribble at pace and centre with precise accuracy, also became a coach, insisting on his teacher's principle of ball control above all else. Injuries had shortened his playing career and he was killed during World War II while suffering in a forced-labour battalion that had been sent to the Russian front.

Having been an inside forward himself, Hogan was particularly proud of Schlosser who epitomised everything he wanted in a creative footballer. In spite of being small and bow-legged, his ball mastery was breathtaking and his finishing excellent. On one occasion he astonished even his coach by scoring six goals for Hungary against Switzerland. The esteem in which he was held was made clear when in 1955 Hungary and Austria played their jubilee match before a crowd of 100,000 in the Nep Stadium, Budapest and he was invited to kick-off. Puskas and Kocsis stood back.

The Austrians lived to regret letting Hogan go to Hungary. Under his guidance the MTK club produced a succession of some of the most powerful teams Europe has ever seen. Between 1916 and 1925, they were not simply champions but virtually unbeatable. And not only that, the massive support for the club brought about the introduction of a fully professional league. It was not inappropriate that a Briton should have such an influence because MTK had been formed in 1888 as an offshoot of the Budapest Gymnastic and Athletic Club, which was started by British people working and living in the city. It certainly profited from those strong British connections.

By the time Hogan had arrived in Hungary, the country's football had already made some positive strides away from their early attempts to raise standards. Curiously, the first goalposts ever used were made in Hungary by a carpenter who built a wooden cage at the back to collect the ball. It was sturdy enough for a visiting goalkeeper from the Richmond club to sit in it and smoke his pipe. Richmond won 4-0 and went on to overcome the local BTC side 6-0.

When looking back, Hogan said: "The time I spent in Hungary was almost as happy as my stay in Austria. Budapest is a lovely city - in my opinion the most beautiful in Europe." There he pinpointed one of the fundamental differences between attitudes to the coaching of young players on the Continent and back in England. He said: "A great advantage which Continental football has over British soccer is that boys are coached in the art of the game from a very tender age in different clubs. There is very little football, if any, played in the schools." In other words even in those far-off days the Hungarian clubs had formed what we would now call "football academies" run by themselves.

Well-meaning though British schoolteachers may have been then, and have remained, only by allowing clubs to coach intensively and regularly will young talent fully blossom. Hogan knew that and it remained one of his firmest of beliefs. He would have approved of the schemes that today's professional clubs run on school pitches throughout Britain, though almost certainly frowned at the number of older foreign players of indifferent standard let loose in the domestic leagues at the expense of home-grown talent.

Many years after England's 1953 defeat by Hungary he made the perceptive remark: "I pay great tribute to the school teachers in England, many of whom are sacrificing any amount of time and trouble to the development of boys' football in this country, but, after all, I state that it is a mere atom as compared with the tremendous amount of work which the fully experienced coaches are putting into their jobs on the Continent. The labour of love which many English teachers are expending with our schoolboys is often undone through their pupils witnessing aimless displays of 'up in the air' football given by some of our professional teams on Saturday afternoons. Boys not only imitate but they also say to themselves: 'The players know how to play the game, it is their profession, but our teachers at school are employed to teach subjects - and football is more of a sideline'."

Writing one of his newspaper articles for the Evening Despatch in 1954, he said: "The average club on the Continent possesses from six to a dozen playing pitches - and the players are divided into four sections, namely: boys, youngsters, juniors and seniors. For instance, when I was coaching in Dresden I had 48 teams and ten playing pitches. The boys are groomed in the basic principles of the game: how to address a ball, trapping, ball control, heading etc, and these exercises are followed by a side game, with the coach or one of his trained assistants in charge. You see, the foreign boy starts in the football school infant class and graduates from that section to the youngster, junior and senior class. Of course some of them don't make the grade and fall by the wayside because they haven't sufficient talent. But this coaching business is marvellous." His own coaching would sometimes involve as many as 100 youths at a time, using twenty footballs. He would form groups of five and move from one to another demonstrating technique.

Having seen his work, a high proportion of the players he taught also took up coaching. Significantly, all of them had been recognised and encouraged by him as highly skilled ball players. Schaffer was particularly successful with his work in foreign countries as well as returning to MTK in the Thirties. All over Europe other clubs took a close interest in what Hogan was achieving with MTK and copied the fluid yet practical way in which they played. Although without doubt the most demanding of taskmasters, his popularity amongst the Hungarian players was immense and the effects of his work won the high regard of officials and spectators. He formulated a way of playing that allowed freedom of expression amongst every single player but without compromising teamwork. However, there is no avoiding the fact that the Continental teams of his day and those of a few decades still to come too often played wonderfully well until they got within shooting range where they lost sight of the game's single most important objective - the scoring of goals. Even so his determination to show that games could be won by stealth and style rather than strength and stamina became the pattern that eventually saw not only the Hungarians of the 1950s but the best of the European club sides reap their rewards.

# PRISON

By stressing that his team had to dictate the pace at which each attack was built he was, in effect, formulating a style of play that had never before been encountered by opponents who attacked with predictable directness and speed. If an attack looked unpromising MTK would suddenly slow down, entice opponents into vulnerable positions and then counter-attack at a sprint. Their formations were never static. Each player was capable of moving into what seemed to be the preserve of another, who in turn found space elsewhere. The ball would often be played carefully but apparently without much sense of purpose across the back or in the middle of the field. Then, suddenly, an attack would form seemingly out of nothing. Opposing defenders would find themselves scuttling back without hope of retrieving the situation. It was the football of a later age - that, in particular, of the lustrous Real Madrid.

In the 1950s the confusion caused in the minds of opponents by the style of play originally taught by Hogan and Meisl was beautifully summed up by the finest football writer of his generation, Geoffrey Green of The Times, when he said that Billy Wright, the England captain in the Wembley defeat, seemed like a fire engine always rushing to the wrong fire. To his immense credit Wright himself often quoted that phrase when trying to explain just how good the Hungarians really were.

# 8

# The Ultimate Insult

DESPITE HAVING BEEN followed around wherever he went by a policeman, Hogan enjoyed his war-time work in Budapest but yearned for the freedom of England. He wrote: "One fine day French troops occupied the lovely city of Budapest and the British landed a small contingent of the Royal Navy from the Danube. Although I had been treated extremely well, it was grand to see our own British sailors. After the armistice had been signed it was some weeks before I could return home to England, and when I eventually did it was on a train guarded by British 'Tommies'." He re-joined his family and they lived with his wife's parents in Burnley. The MTK players were saddened by his departure and in the spirit of the "smoking is good for you" advertising of the time bought him an inscribed cigarette lighter: "To Our Dearest Bacsi with best wishes - the thankful MTK players".

The pleasure of his return home was tempered by the knowledge that in austere times there would be few calls for a football coach. Fortunately, while in Hungary he had become friendly with Gordon Walker, the owner of Walker's Tobacco Co. Walker, who had often shared food parcels with him as Hogan was not allowed them since being without a passport he was considered not to have a country of origin, arranged for him to have a job as a dispatch foreman in Liverpool. The family found accommodation in Knotty Ash. The sad irony was that while he was grateful for the work, it also encouraged the smoking that eventually led to his death from emphysema.

Money was still extremely short and he was advised to go to the Football Association headquarters in London to apply for help from a special fund that had been set up to give relief to professionals who had suffered financially during the war years. He even had to borrow five pounds for the train fare. His hope was that he would be given the £200 he had heard was likely to be available and be able to set up a business of his own, though quite what he had in mind he kept to himself.

When he arrived at the FA headquarters in London he was treated as a complete stranger. After a long wait in the entrance hall he met the Secretary, Frederick Wall, who quickly destroyed his optimism by saying that he was not eligible for any money at all. Hogan pleaded. Wall sneered. The fund, he said, was intended to assist men who had gone to war. Hogan protested that he had never been given the opportunity to fight because he had been interned when war was declared and detained in Austria and Hungary.

Wall suggested that they continued their conversation more privately in his office. There his manner became less aggressive. He said he was well aware of Hogan's record as a coach. Hogan began to think that in spite of the earlier conversation there might be an offer of a future job or at least some financial assistance. Instead, Wall went to a cupboard and found three pairs of khaki woollen socks; "These will help you, Hogan. We used to send them to the boys at the front and I know they were very grateful." For once in his life Hogan was at a loss for words, appalled at what was a clear accusation that he had deliberately avoided military service and was, in effect, a traitor. The fact that he had been detained abroad without any chance of returning to volunteer for war service was obviously not considered sufficient reason to have failed to join the forces. Thereafter his relationship with the FA remained cool.

# PROPHET OR TRAITOR?

To put Wall's attitude into perspective, he had lost several close relatives in the war and that must not only have dictated his behaviour towards Hogan but led to his distrust of anything Continental. In international affairs his attitude was that FIFA needed England more than England needed FIFA.

After the setback in London Hogan was sorely tempted to get out of football altogether. Britain was only slowly recovering its normality. Jobs were scarce. Football coaches were not high on the list of required workers. In desperation he wrote to several Continental clubs. He heard that F.C. Young Boys Berne in Switzerland were interested in finding a new coach. They invited him for an interview. So, in 1921, he was again travelling back into Europe in search of employment. He liked the look of the city and its club. He was taken on and the club's officials and players soon took to him. After three months coaching with them he sent for his family. His children went to a local school and quickly picked up German, which was spoken locally. They then helped him by interpreting what he could not understand himself.

He spent two successful years with the Young Boys club, coaching them to become runners-up in the national league and at the same time he taught the club's six junior teams. He also trained the Swiss national side who had two notable successes, a 5-0 win over Holland in Berne and a 2-2 draw with Italy in Bologna. Both results made the rest of the Continent not only take notice of little Switzerland but renew their interest in the coach and his methods. Four of the national side came from his Young Boys club. As a result he was in demand to do coaching sessions with the best players from all over the country.

After their second year in Switzerland his wife thought it was time to find a place where the children could have a sound education. As a result in 1924 he accepted the position as trainer to Lausanne Sports FC and the children became fluent in French. The club finished high in the league table but his

86

pride was hurt when he discovered that the championship winners, Servette, were coached by a former Blackpool and Blackburn player, Thomas Crook Duckworth.

Back in Austria Meisl was still following Hogan's guidelines. The Scottish style, with its strong emphasis on ball control and inventive passing, remained his template. Even so there were times when he was tempted to give in to a more direct style of play. Not long after the First World War had ended, Austria went to Nuremberg to play Southern Germany. On an icy pitch, their attempts to concentrate on a short passing, always-accurate game failed. Dwelling on the fact that the Germans had scored five without reply from Austria, Meisl and his team spent the long journey home debating whether or not it was time to think of strength and directness as the better way. They came to the conclusion that they should remain true to their principles and those precepts formed the bedrock on which was built the remarkable "Wunderteam".

Although his work in Lausanne was agreeable enough, Hogan was always hankering after a return to Hungary and perhaps more in the way of remuneration (he continued to send money back to England to assist members of the family who were out of work). The invitation came early in 1925. It was an offer without the possibility of refusal. Hungaria F.C., the new name for MTK, asked him if he could go back to join them in Budapest. He immediately signed a two-year contract but the family stayed in Lausanne. In his absence MTK had first declined then made a recovery to regain their place as a considerable strength. He rapidly got back into the routine of coaching everyone from the youths to the seniors. The work lasted for two years and he felt that he could have stayed forever. He adored the city and in later life was saddened to think how it had changed in character under the oppressive Communist regime, which he hated. With the advantage of his guidance the club won the national championship and cup.

# PROPHET OR TRAITOR?

While he was in Budapest there was an international football conference during which he was approached by Hans Hadlicke, president of the Central German Football Association, who was interested in appointing him as senior coach. Hogan had always anticipated that, sooner or later, Germany would become a major force in international football, so he responded positively. The suggested contract was attractive. The money exceeded anything he had received before. However, it was less than a decade since the First World War and he was concerned about the attitude of Germans to having a British coach, let alone the response of people at home. He was assured that any bitterness after the War had long since disappeared; nevertheless he decided to send his children back to England while he and his wife moved to Jena.

At his first meeting with the committee of the Central German FA in Leipzig he was told that his job would be to tour all over the country giving lectures about coaching. Naturally, they insisted that he had to teach in German. While he could hold a basic conversation in the language he was still far from fluent. He confessed that to the committee members but they seemed unconcerned and told him to go to Zwickau in a fortnight. Clubs from the area would send their players, along with other coaches and managers to study his methods. Each morning he was to teach schoolboys. In the evenings a hall would be hired and the idea was that he would lecture in German. Looking back at his time in the country he said: "I think of all the countries in which I worked as a coach Germany was the most interesting and the most industrious." But his stay began badly.

Knowing that his command of German was inadequate, he asked to be allowed to write his lectures and let someone else translate them into German. He had a lot of keen listeners since there were more men and boys playing football in that country

88

than any other in the world. One club in Hamburg had over 100 teams. Unknown to him, his arrival in Zwickau coincided with a political battle between the German FA and the National Gymnastics Association. Both wanted to encourage youngsters to follow their own particular sports. When he got to the railway station he was met by a delegation from the Central German FA, all in frock coats and top hats. He said he had not expected such a welcome and that it was not necessary, to which they replied that it was for "propaganda" reasons - it may well have been the first time he had ever heard the word that was to become so familiar on the approach to another world war.

His coaching work at schools, with teachers translating, started well. The afternoon sessions with the older players were more of a problem. He coached in his usual way, emphasising the importance of ball work and giving demonstrations. He organised training matches, occasionally interrupting to point out mistakes. At the end of the first session one of the German FA officials came up to him and said that while the coaching was all very well there was nothing in it that he had not seen demonstrated by Dr. Otto Nerz, who was the powerful head coach of their own association and assistant national team manager. Hogan saw the threat to his future and confused his critic by saying that his method of coaching was not to give away too much too soon. The official seemed happy but the committee was inclined to think that Hogan was coming over too strongly as a non-German speaker, which had already annoyed several of the other coaches.

He was given an ultimatum: give a lecture in German without any assistance before an audience of about five hundred, which included Dr. Nerz, or resign. He planned to deflect attention away from his language deficiency by introducing himself as a professor of football rather a master of languages. Embarrassingly, he got this the wrong way round and quickly had the audience laughing at him rather than with him. He ploughed on. He tried to say that football was an exercise for the mind as well as the body, but the word he used for "mind" was actually "committee". He recalled that it was perhaps only his inherited Irish stubbornness that made him determined to continue. Mistake followed mistake until the audience was convulsed in laughter. It was a fiasco needing a desperate recovery. He came to the conclusion that the only way to win them over was to do what he had always done with such confidence and skill.

He called for a ten-minute intermission and quickly went to find his football kit, which was still the Bolton Wanderers strip. On his return he asked for an interpreter. He got a ball and bravely told the audience that three-quarters of the German players he had seen could not even kick it properly. He said they toe punted and still had their boots made with reinforced toes (as did the British players of the time, who continued to do so long after most players on the Continent had realised that softer boots offered much greater feel for the ball). He told them that heavy boots did nothing for ball control. He took off his own as well as his socks. He placed the ball on the floor and said he intended to hit a narrow panel in a wall some fifteen yards away, which he did with his right foot, splitting the wood from top to bottom.

He noticed that he had kicked so hard that his foot was bleeding. He then made the absurd claim that all British players were two footed. So he took aim with his bare left foot and an even fiercer shot completely smashed the wall panel. While the audience stood and roared its approval, he looked down at a pool of blood.

He continued to demonstrate other skills and, with typical bravado, later claimed that he was "never an inch out". Swelling in confidence as well as in pain from his swollen feet, he decided that it was time to show Dr. Nerz "a thing or two".

# THE ULTIMATE INSULT

He asked one of the best local players to join him on the stage and completely bemused him by running the ball at him after asking him to intercept. He beat his mesmerised opponent with hypnotic body swerves. The local Burgomaster said he had never before seen anything as entertaining on his local stage.

With his reputation rescued and again beginning to go ahead of him, he went touring the towns and villages more as an entertainer than football coach. He liked nothing better than an appreciative audience and later developed his "lectures" into something approaching a stage show. In a single month in Dresden he gave demonstrations to more than 5,000 players. In one small village he taught 450 and he stayed for fourteen days in Chemnitz, instructing 2,500. There he happened to meet Norman Dickenson who had been with Bolton Wanderers on their original tour of Holland. Like Hogan, he had taken his skill abroad but his was as a yarn merchant.

They went to Hogan's favourite restaurant to reminisce and ate bear cutlets. Over the meal Hogan admitted that he was concerned that several of the best visiting British amateur teams, which in those days ought to have been stronger than the top sides Germany could produce, had been made to look ordinary. Even Cambridge University were hammered 6-1 by Hamburg Sport Vereine. He warned any other visiting clubs from Britain that there were "no longer any cake walks here".

In later years his "act" as a ball juggler entertained Second World War troops and was highly popular but his priority in Germany remained the finding of promising players and the honing of their skills. He discovered Richard Hofmann playing football in the village of Meerene in West Saxony and turned him into such a splendid player that he became known in the national Press as the "greatest German footballer of all time". Hofmann, an inside forward, played twenty-five times for Germany and scored twenty-four goals.

# PROPHET OR TRAITOR?

Although Hogan made only a fleeting visit to Meerene, he left Hofmann a training schedule and told him that if he followed the instructions he would become an international. They met several times more and after following the advice Hofmann was chosen for the Central German team. Meanwhile, Hogan had become more friendly with Dr. Nerz, to whom he recommended Hofmann for the national side itself. Meanwhile, his contract expired and he was again on the move. His work in Germany had involved coaching forty-six different teams from under twelves to seniors. Because football was not played at school level, the clubs took responsibility. Hamburg SV had 120 teams. He had been in his element, bringing on players from a young age.

An offer to coach the Dresden club became attractive, mainly because he was confident that he could persuade Hofmann to join him as a part-time professional. The move worked and Hofmann developed into an even more imposing striker, regularly scoring three or more goals in international matches. Playing against Sweden he got the ball in the net six times but three of the "goals" were disallowed by a referee who seemed to be feeling sorry for the outclassed Swedes.

# 9

# Duty Calls

IN SPITE OF HIS LONG EXPERIENCE abroad, Hogan never lost his sense of duty to the "old country". Shortly before England played against Germany in the 1930 match, he travelled to Berlin to meet the players. "I thought it was my duty to warn the England skipper, David Jack, that Hofmann would be a considerable threat." They met and Jack said he had already heard how dangerous Hofmann was and that England had asked a Sheffield Wednesday player, Alf Strange, to mark him. Hogan introduced himself to Strange who sounded confident, but Hogan told him that if he allowed Hofmann a yard of space he would regret it. Strange, who had won only two previous caps, said: "We'll see."

. On the morning before the match the Sporting Life published an article by Hogan warning England of the problems they were likely to face against Germany and in the game against Austria in Vienna four days later. He attempted to write in a patriotic vein, but there was no doubting the fact that he thought England's confidence could be misplaced.

He explained: "It is about twenty years since an English international side visited these countries. In the meantime football has improved wonderfully and the British League teams have often suffered defeat. The general opinion out here is that foreign football is now better than British, and that England will lose both games. But good judges are well aware that British football has still no superior, and these 'old heads' are expecting England to triumph. But nothing has been left undone in the preparation of the Continental teams. For instance, in Germany during the past few months lectures on football and practical demonstrations have been held in Duisberg, Nurnberg and Breslau. New players have been discovered and several important trial games have been played in order to select the strongest team."

On the following day in front of a full house England sent out a powerful side: Hibbs; Goodall, Blenkinsop; Strange, Webster, Marsden; Crooks, Jack, Watson, Bradford, Rimmer. Hogan felt awkward sitting with the German officials, but they were his employers. "England started to play some copybook football so I sat back, lit a cigar and relaxed." England took the lead but then, some twenty-five yards out, Hofmann controlled a loose ball on his chest in exactly the way Hogan had demonstrated so often. He moved it forward with his left foot and hit in a searing long shot with his right. Hibbs, probably the best goalkeeper in the world between the wars, admitted that he did not move an inch.

A terrible collision left Marsden badly hurt and although he played out the rest of the half on the wing, his career was as good as finished. England led 2-1 at the interval but had to play the second half with ten men. Twenty minutes into the half Hofmann hit another unstoppable shot past Hibbs. Ten minutes from time and it was again Hofmann who took possession and broke through England's defence. Hibbs came out and dived at his feet. Instantly Hofmann lifted the ball over him with the outside of his foot. Hogan confessed: "I had known with a mixture of elation and national sorrow, that the moment he approached Hibbs, the goal was a certainty."

The German crowd could not contain its excitement but almost at the end Webster made a long run out of the England defence and refused to pass the ball to colleagues, who were screaming at him to release it. Hogan was on his feet while the Germans around sat rigid with worried anticipation. Webster got to the penalty area before passing to Crooks on the wing. Crooks centred perfectly for Jack to head in the equaliser. Almost at once the referee called a memorable 3-3 draw to a close. Hogan felt justified in his warning about Hofmann. Jack agreed and so, reluctantly, did Strange.

In spite of his show of patriotism in Berlin, his stay with Dresden was enormously popular and successful. At the same time he was also hopeful that one of his sons, Joe, would make the grade as a professional player. Joe had been signed on by Racing Club, in France, as an outside right but never made a fruitful career in the game.

During Hogan's first season with Dresden the team were not only unbeaten but did not drop a single point. In the next they were again unbeaten although drew three games, and in the third they lost one match and conceded a draw. Hogan blamed himself for the one defeat by Guts Muts who were also challenging for the championship, explaining that he planned to drop the regular goalkeeper who was a commercial traveller and had not been appearing for training. However, the goalkeeper turned up on the Thursday night and in spite of his doubts about the player's fitness and attitude Hogan changed his mind and selected him.

On the Saturday of the championship decider the goalkeeper failed to appear and Dresden played the first ten minutes without one, until a loudspeaker announcement to the crowd brought the young reserve scurrying into the dressing room. He was petrified. The first shot he had to deal with went over his head and into the goal, leaving him lying on the ground seemingly in a dead faint; but Dresden won, and with it the title. In the following season they again played against Guts Muts for the trophy and had to face the most notoriously physical centre-forward in Germany, Sackenheim. Hogan had decided that for the first time in his career he would ask his centre half to play as a third back, which worked so well that Dresden won 6-0 and again took the championship. He and the players were given gold commemorative watches. So in all three years Dresden were champions of both East Saxony and Central Germany.

The Dresden Sports Club in 1928 had 1,000 members, five grounds and fourteen teams. By the time he left there were 1,750 members, nine grounds and forty-three teams. The progress was phenomenal but at the same time he continued to worry about the fact that he was coaching players who might one day show that English football standards were in decline. He was impressed with the comparatively high financial investment the Germans were prepared to make in the game and the responsibility they were ready to invest in the coaches. He said that the work of a trainer in Britain could not be compared with that of his Continental counterpart: "There are no such things as 'rubbing down', looking after the boots etc as in England. Here we have special men for attending to these matters. The trainer's work here is to teach the game."

On occasions he would have a coaching session with local players in the town, then organise a match for which he would be referee. He had noticed that many of the players were heavy smokers and in spite of his own smoking habit he regularly warned them about the likely damage to their health. In one match he was about to blow the whistle for the kick-off when he noticed that one of his linesmen was smoking. He bellowed at him "Cigarette", to which the linesman shouted back, "Please excuse me Mr Trainer, I can't offer you one, this is the last one I have".

In newspaper interviews he continued to send his warnings about the threat Continental football posed to the game at home. In one he said: "I have watched Continental football grow from a mere baby to a strong lad and develop into a strapping young man. The question is: will it reach the stage of full-grown manhood and eventually deprive Britain of her football supremacy? That remains to be seen. We were once the world-beaters in other branches of sport. Years ago if one had forecast the French as future world champions in tennis, such a person would have been locked up. Yet it has come to pass, not only in tennis but very nearly in rugby football, too. This wonderful improvement hasn't been accomplished by work on the running tracks! When I think of the early days out here, of players who were only able to kick with one foot, afraid of heading the ball, no idea of trapping or ball control and so on, and then realise that out of such material a team has been produced to beat our crack team, Newcastle United 4-0. Well, it makes one rub one's eyes." He accused British players of being "far too cocky and conceited, always thinking that when we get into a first-class team we have nothing else to learn".

He said that his work in Germany was "strenuous" which was an understatement. Even so, he was greatly encouraged by the enthusiasm not only of the players but the public. Describing one of his coaching tours he said: "There has been gratitude all along the line. I arrived once in a little town in lovely Thuringia and found two hundred people on the railway station. I had no idea that they were waiting to give me a good reception. On many occasions the Lord Mayor has honoured me with his presence at my football lectures, which is a sure sign that everybody is in earnest and willing to learn the game. The youngsters are so keenly interested that they often form a procession and accompany the trainer from his hotel to the ground, but, of course, there are exceptions.

"I have come across the football stars or 'Cannons', as they are called in Germany, who think they have nothing to learn; but these are few and far between. The £10,000 English player David Jack, who has had very much experience of Continental football, in an article in All Sports has expressed the opinion

# PROPHET OR TRAITOR?

that South American football is for the moment the best abroad, but states that he is willing to wager on Germany for the future, and that the Fatherland will play a very important part if ever we have a world football championship." Prophetic, indeed.

Hogan's attention to detail was keen to the point of being a fixation. His obsession with the importance of trapping, which he repeatedly said was something English first division footballers failed to accomplish with much reliability, led to his producing a series of exercises which he insisted all players under his instruction had to carry out. Most of it now seems obvious but it should have been essential for trainers back in England at the time, especially those who had no time for Hogan's insistence that players had to have a "feel" for the ball and know how to use their bodies to make the ball submit. Wherever he went he showed his pupils a list of eleven ways to control the ball:

1. The pupils form a square, consisting of four persons, and throw or kick the ball to one another. The sole of the foot must first be put on the ball with the weight of the body resting on the other foot. This is the simple trapping exercise, which teaches the pupil how to time the ball. With continuous exercise the pupil at length becomes able to take one look at the ball, and the moment he traps it he can glance at the position of his opponent. At the same time, it is explained by the trainer that it seldom happens during the modern football game that a player has so much time to trap the ball in this manner; nevertheless, it is a splendid exercise.

2. Trapping the ball with the inside of the foot. This is more practical because it teaches the pupil how to gather the ball on the run without losing any time. Some of the experts are able to do this kind of trapping with the instep, but the surer method is with the inside of the foot.

# DUTY CALLS

3. Trapping and pushing the ball at once to a comrade, the ball to be kept low. It is an exercise which requires any amount of practice before precision is attained.

4. Trapping the ball on the turn. Very important. This is really the most practical way of trapping the ball in modern football. The upper part of the leg must be lifted in dog-like fashion, the ball taken with the inside of the foot, a sudden turn, and the player is on the run with the ball in his possession.

5. Trapping with the outside of the foot. It is as well to note that all trapping, passing and ball control exercises must be done with the right foot and the left so that it doesn't trouble the player to control the ball no matter how it comes to him.

6. Trapping or stopping the ball with the head and bringing it down to one's feet. The average player is better with his feet than his head and sometimes one is inclined to head when it is not necessary. Especially is this the case when the opponent is not near. Such a ball must be brought down to the feet to give the player a better opportunity of placing it. The exercise is performed by letting the body and head give way and tucking the latter into the shoulders at the last moment - resistance will only send the ball away out of control.

7. Trapping the ball and bringing it down with the chest. The body gives way at the moment of contact with the ball, being careful to keep the arms out of the way.

8. Trapping in the region of the stomach. The body gives way at the moment of contact with the ball and forming a sort of bridge or basket, like a cricket ball dropping into the hand.

9. Taking the ball lower. The ball is taken on the thigh by lifting the knee a little and the thigh giving way at the moment of contact.

10. Trapping a very low ball. Take the ball on the instep by letting it give way. This is more an exercise for giving the pupil the delicate touch of the ball and is hardly practical during the game.

# PROPHET OR TRAITOR?

11. This is rather more difficult to explain but is sometimes useful for the outside right or left. For instance, the outside right, on the run, receives a bad pass, the ball, instead of being pushed forward, comes a little in the rear. With the left foot forward and the right foot behind, the ball can be gathered and pushed forward by the inside of the latter foot. This takes a bit of doing, but everything can be done by practice, and we are great believers in ball work on the Continent.

He continued to express his concern for the future of the game back home. "Many of our First Division teams have been hopelessly beaten on the Continent, and to make matters worse an amateur team from Berlin has crossed over to England and beaten a strong Isthmian League team by 4-1. Naturally such results make one ask what is the matter with British football? Something is radically wrong, that is a certainty. Otherwise how do you account for the fact that foreign teams, with whom we used to wipe the floor, are now practically doing the same with English teams?

"The foreigner is not a natural football player; the game has been drilled into him by old British coaches. Another thing, football on the Continent has had to fight hard for its very existence on account of the competition of other national games. In Germany, for instance, football was strictly forbidden in the schools, and this is still the case in many parts of the country. The very foundations of the game were attacked and undermined, yet, despite these handicaps, teams have been produced to defeat our best sides. It is about time we woke up and realised the state of affairs so that we can put our house in order again.

"Home football and the players' preparations are wrong from the very foundations. Take the boy at school, for instance. He gets plenty of football practice of a sort, 'shooting in', but in the whole of my experience in England I never saw a teacher showing the boys how to pass a ball, how to trap, how to control or how to head. The boy's natural talent for the game is never really developed when he is young, and what happens to him when he becomes a First League player? His training consists of walking, running and skipping. The only ball training he gets is the beloved 'shooting in'.

"Such a thing as theoretical lessons on the blackboard about positions, play and so on are practically unheard of in England. The very idea would be laughed to scorn by many of the players. In the meantime we are suffering defeats by foreign teams who are trained in this manner.

"All of this requires any amount of work and noble sacrifice. In Switzerland and Hungary, for instance, I have often been at the ground at 7 a.m until 8 p.m and in many countries we play football during eleven months of the year. In England the time has come for us to change our methods otherwise all will be lost. We must alter our training system and introduce more exercises for ball control, a thing that seems to be a lost art in present-day English football. Let us have a little theoretical work, discussions about the game, arranging of plans, and so on."

# 10

# Escape to Freedom

THE GERMAN LEAGUE championship was won for a fourth season. Among the promising young players he encouraged was Helmut Schoen who later managed the elegant West German side that recovered from being defeated by England in 1966 to win the 1972 European Championship and went on to become world champions in 1974. He said that in every coaching session he would have in his mind the advice he had received from Hogan.

Everything at Dresden seemed to be going well until the political upheaval of the early thirties began to touch the lives of everyone in the country. At the same time, yet again Hogan came into conflict with club officials over requests for more money. He took the advice of Meisl, who because of his Jewish background was deeply concerned about the growth of fascism in Germany, and decided it was an opportune moment to move on. Again Meisl worked behind the scenes to smooth his way forward by arranging for him to be interviewed by Racing Club de Paris, but it was not as simple as that.

Dresden gave the family a lavish and warm send off but Hogan was deeply worried about getting out of Germany and into France with sufficient money to set them up in a new country. He had the equivalent of just two hundred pounds to his name but the German government had ordered that considerably less than that could be taken out of the country.

# ESCAPE TO FREEDOM

His daughter, Mary, suggested a way to smuggle out all of the money. She said that her father should change his cash into large 1,500 Mark notes, which he did. She then took the stitches out of the pleats of the plus-four trousers which her father and the two boys wore at the time, hid the notes and stitched them back.

The family took the train to the German-French border. There a German patrol came on board and moved slowly though each compartment. Every single passenger was searched. Coats had to be removed and even shoes. Hogan attempted to make conversation with the armed guards but he admitted "the perspiration was just running down my back". They demanded that all bags were opened. They were fooled. The money remained undiscovered. Once the train had moved into France the relief amongst the Hogan family could not be concealed. He remembered: "As we passed over the frontier - with me and my two lads sitting safely on our little Bank of England - we gave three hearty British cheers." They joined another train and joyfully felt free.

His time in Germany had been rewarding and was appreciated. So much so that perhaps it is as well that a letter from the German football association to his son Frank has never previously been revealed. Although Hogan was indisputably loyal to his home country, the fact is that not only in Hungary did he start the cogs turning in what was to become the Continent's challenge to the theory of England's supremacy, but in Germany, too. That groundwork eventually led to the rise in world football of their power, which, in spite of 1966, has so regularly frustrated England in international competition. When Hogan died in 1974, the General Secretary of the German football association, Hans Passlack, said in his letter to Frank that Hogan had been the founder of "modern football" in his country and that they owed the ensuing results to him. Were it not for the fact that English football had such little interest in coaching and what Hogan could offer, that tribute could have been interpreted as more evidence of a man who had reneged on his own country.

Finally the family got to Paris. With his reputation again preparing the way, it was only a matter of days before Racing Club de France, who were involved in the first season of professional football in France (they were previously more famous for tennis and had Jean Borotra as a member), got in touch. But there was competition for the coaching vacancy. Among those being considered was David Jack, by now an experienced coach but like Hogan forced to work abroad. The club had ample funds. It was supported by a millionaire, Jean Bernard Levy, and could have enticed anyone they wanted. They chose Hogan.

The French first division clubs had each been permitted to sign four foreign players. Chelsea's Andy Wilson and Alec Cheyne were already with Racing and Hogan was allowed to travel home to England to seek out two others he was sure would be useful: Freddie Kennedy (Manchester United and Everton) and Fred Phoenix (Aston Villa) who were known to be keen on playing abroad. Both signed. He then got in touch with contacts in Hungary to obtain the country's best centre half, Emilio Berkessy. As the new squad of players began to converge, the British contingent was led by Kennedy who, to the amusement of the rest, got off the train in Paris wearing a bowler hat and carrying an umbrella.

Hogan's real coup was to obtain one of the finest goalkeepers of all time, the Austrian Rudi Hiden whom the Arsenal manager Herbert Chapman badly wanted to sign. Curiously it was Hogan's friend and colleague Meisl who had attempted to prepare the way for Hiden to join Arsenal. He arranged for the transfer fee of £2,000 to be deposited in an Austrian bank and Hiden had actually left Vienna, but he was not allowed to get into Britain because the labour regulations in force at the time stated that anyone entering the country could not receive a labour (work) permit until they had been a resident for two years. Arsenal were furious.

To Hogan's slight embarrassment, Hiden had no choice but to forget Arsenal and accept his offer to move to Paris. The goalkeeper took on French nationality and later represented his adopted country. After his playing career was over he moved to Italy and managed several clubs, returning to Austria just before the Second World War. His life ended in sad circumstances. In 1968 he fell ill and needed to have a leg amputated. Because he had defected to France he was not able to draw a state pension and so ended his days in comparative poverty.

Kennedy proved particularly popular with the fans in Paris but Phoenix suffered a cruel fate. He had always talked of Arsenal's Cliff Bastin as his hero, so it was sadly ironic that when Racing Club went to Highbury to meet Arsenal in a friendly match, he broke his leg while marking him.

Hogan found that having a millionaire club owner in Levy had its downside: "He would spoil the players with money and gifts so that discipline became impossible." After every match Levy treated all of them to a slap-up hotel dinner, whether or not they had won. Hogan was horrified and felt that the players were being given far too many opportunities to lose fitness and dedication. He personally was still fanatical about keeping fit, maintaining a healthy diet and continuing to exercise daily well into his eighties.

The lack of discipline worried him so much that although he had agreed to stay with the club for two years, he began to realise that he was not making much progress. Coaching the British and other imported players was no problem but he found the French much more difficult. His opinionated attitude was not for them, although he remarked that there was nothing wrong with their potential. Indeed, in later years, he occasionally acted as chief instructor to the French FA in Rheims and was always satisfied with the dedication of the French players, which had markedly improved.

In his first season with Racing they finished runners-up, but all was not well within the family. His daughter Mary had been unwell and he was also beginning to despair of the French players' lack of respect for his strict code of behaviour. Yet again, and despite the fact that he was being paid better than at any previous time in his career, he decided that what he called the "Hogan family circus" should move on. Quite reasonably the club asked him to find a replacement coach, which he did. Curtis Booth, who had been with Newcastle United, took over and Hogan chose to move back to Lausanne where he re-joined the club he had left eight years previously. By now Joe was a fairly experienced player while Frank was a member of the Lausanne junior side and but for a later serious lung problem could have been a successful player.

As a postscript to Hogan's time with Racing, and another poor reflection on English football's insularity, in the 1950s, when Hogan was coaching at Aston Villa, Emilio Berkessy paid a visit. After his playing career had ended he became a respected coach and gave several members of the 1953 Hungarian side (not least the incomparable Hidegkuti) that beat England their early instruction in the game. However, in 1948 he decided that politics was playing too large a part in football and managed to get out of the country. He coached in Italy and Spain but found himself out of work and visited Villa to seek the advice of Hogan. He could not return to Hungary and desperately wanted to join an English club, but in spite of his experience and Hogan's efforts on his behalf only Grimsby Town showed any interest. And even that appointment soon became lost in the red tape of a refused work permit.

The Lausanne club provided the Hogan family with a big house on the edge of Lake Geneva with views of the mountains. In many ways it was the happiest period in the lives of the entire family. The years of upheaval had put a strain on all of them and the tranquillity of the situation was therapeutic. Hogan said, "To be frank I could have stayed there for the rest of my life," but there were difficulties within the club itself which had recently turned professional.

Lausanne had been struggling before he arrived but the first season brought moderately good results. However, his determined independence again got him into awkward situations. The chairman continually demanded explanations about team selection. "He was a grocer and should have stuck to his trade," Hogan complained. "He thought he knew everything about football but what he really knew you could write on the back of a half-penny stamp." He particularly disliked the chairman appearing at training, criticising the players and suggesting that they should be fined for any mistakes, especially missed goals. "That made my thoughts turn to home."

Both sons were well into their twenties and though they had the benefit of a good and international education (both spoke several languages), he was concerned that they had no professions outside football. Neither son could be sure that the sport would provide a living in the long term. Their sister, never one to be slow in giving an opinion, pointed out to her father that the "boys" would be better off back in England. It was agreed, but Hogan himself continued to roam wherever there was work. He even spent a short time coaching in North Africa where he discovered that the local players had such good ball control that he predicted: "One day they will show us all a thing or two." And so they have.

Back in England the country's obstinate superiority complex remained in good health. As far ago as 1929 the football authorities should have had doubts driven into their minds. On a sweltering May Day in Madrid, England suffered a 4-3 defeat by a Spanish side that gave them a lesson in dribbling. It was the first time the countries had met and England badly wanted a quick return match in order to get their revenge. The Spaniards were keen to retain their proud, new-found status as long as they could and avoided England until December, 1931. They went, somewhat reluctantly, to Highbury and were thumped 7-0, a result that confirmed in the minds of most England fans and officials that perhaps the loss in Spain had been one of those freaks occasionally seen in the world game and had a lot to do with the weather. Undoubtedly, that was not entirely true.

Writing in the Sporting Life as early as November, 1929, Hogan had said: "The average football enthusiast in England, reading of a defeat of a British team abroad, just chuckles to himself and probably remarks, 'Well, I suppose the boys have been having a good time, and that accounts for it'. Very little does he ponder over the reasons for the disastrous defeats of Huddersfield Town, Newcastle United, Bolton Wanderers and the English international side itself during their Continental tours last spring. On the Continent it was once a case of 'only British trainers required' but of late things have changed. Owing to the poor displays and defeats of our touring sides, the foreign football coach has suddenly sprung into existence, and now easily outnumbers his British rival. It is quite a common thing, after the reverse of a British eleven, say, in Budapest or Vienna, for the Continental clubs to engage an Austrian or Hungarian trainer in preference to the Britisher, who is left out in the cold."

Reiterating his belief in the teaching and daily practice of ball control, he said: "As boys at school we learnt how to play the game by kicking the ball every day for hours upon hours, and it seems strange to me that when we become First League players ball work is dropped like hot bricks and we are trained for the game on the running tracks or on the golf links. No wonder that many an English League player is unable to trap the ball properly. I am British and proud of it, but I must be candid and express the opinion that there is now very little difference between British and foreign football. Perhaps there is just a little margin in our favour. The results speak for themselves. Defeats of British sides are far too frequent. Such excuses as tired teams, travelling, bad referees, etc. are too trivial. Compared with these, I must say that the foreign football player never has a rest, plays more games, and travels quite as much as his British cousin.

"The truth about the matter is, the football players abroad are better prepared for the game, and the secret of this is ball practice and theoretical instructions. I know that I shall be treading on some people's toes when I say that British football training methods are out of date, and Austria and Germany are waiting quietly to prove this when the English international eleven tours the Continent."

Meanwhile Meisl, encouraged by Hogan's earlier work, had continued to build a special Austrian national eleven (the "Wunderteam"), a side to be considered alongside the best in any era of world football. While the English game was now firmly dominated by the thinking of Chapman and his Arsenal team, with their "stopper" centre-half defensive tactic and W-M formation (two full-backs, a centre-back, two half-backs linking with two deep lying inside forwards, a centre-forward and two wingers), elsewhere the earlier 2-3-5, or pyramid, system was still popular, particularly with the Austrians. Not only that, both teams in the first World Cup final (1930), Argentina and Uruguay, utilised the old pattern to good effect. Indeed, internationally it took the inventiveness of Italy's Vittorio Pozzo to break its hold when he adapted it, putting more emphasis on the defensive responsibilities of the inside forwards. Whereas Hogan had always encouraged attacking by stealth and accuracy, Pozzo promoted the fast, surprise counter-attack. The style led to one writer to say: "The other team does all the attacking, but Italy win the game." Nothing changes.

Chapman did not live long enough to continue with his own innovations but there is little doubt that had he survived, his Arsenal would have continued to be at the forefront of tactical evolution. Yet, mysteriously, The Times correspondent Geoffrey Green wrote in his 1953 book Soccer The World Game: "I believe it is true to say that Herbert Chapman was preparing once more to spring a surprise on football by switching back to something like the old formation when he died! Once everyone had followed him as though he were the Pied Piper and no doubt they would have done so again." Chapman died in 1934 having had only one opportunity to influence English football at international level. He was allowed to be the figurehead manager of England for a match against Italy in Rome in 1933. The game ended in a 1-1 draw. Chapman had been allowed to give a pre-match talk and another at half-time, but in all other respects he was under the thumb of the FA whose committee members chose the team.

Although Chapman was more pragmatic than Hogan, they were at one in their views about coaching. Not long after the match in Italy he wrote: "The idea may be startling. But I would like the English selectors to choose twenty of the most promising young players in the game and arrange for them to be brought together once a week, under a selector, a coach and a trainer. The object of this would be to enable them to go out and practice with definite schemes planned. If this proposal were carried out, I think the result would be astonishing. I may say I have no hope of this international building policy being adopted, but it is on these new lines that some of the Continental countries are working." Less than a year later Chapman succumbed to pneumonia.

In the two years prior to meeting England at Stamford

# ESCAPE TO FREEDOM

Bridge in 1932, "old fashioned" tactics or not, the Austrians not only held England to a goalless draw in Vienna (1930) but showed such shrewd organisation that in the following year Scotland were easily beaten 5-0. That match against the Scots can be seen as the first serious notification that world football was about to see a very special international side. Most people in Vienna had assumed that their team would be beaten by a considerable margin. As a result the attendance of some 40,000 was low by the standards of the time. However, the journalist Ivan Sharpe commented that the performance by the Austrians was even better than the one he had seen from the famous Scottish "Blue Wizards" against England at Wembley in 1928 when they won 5-1.

At their peak, Austria went on to thrash Germany 6-0 and 5-0, Switzerland were overcome 8-1 and 3-1, also Italy 2-1 and Hungary 8-2. The defeat of Hungary saw probably the finest performance of Matthias Sindelar's career. He was involved in every significant attack, scored three himself and he had a say in all of the other goals. This amazing Austrian side played thirteen consecutive international games without defeat, winning ten and drawing the remainder.

The Continent had never produced such a complete and artistic group. It was inevitable that when they came to play against England on December 7, 1932 the match would be labelled the unofficial championship of Europe. More than that, though, it should have shocked English football into accepting that everything that Hogan had said about its failure to recognise the fast-growing power of the Continent was true.

# 11

# His Greatest Honour

HOGAN WAS ASKED BY the Austrian federation whether he would join Meisl, the manager, in acting as trainer to the national team for the 1932 game in London and, in spite of his usual feeling of mixed loyalties, there was not the slightest chance of his turning them down. To take them to England was what he described as "the greatest honour of my football career, and a magnificent present for my fiftieth birthday". The Austrians were under no misapprehension that however skillful their side had become, playing England in England would still be a huge challenge. The Spanish side that had done so well to beat the English in Madrid in 1929 had then suffered the 7-1 humiliating defeat at Highbury in 1931. It was obvious that on home soil England were still an imposing force.

Hogan and Meisl feared that England would again be in an uncompromising mood. Yet they were also aware that England's seemingly comfortable win over Spain possibly said as much about Spanish nerves as English superiority. Indeed, a few days after the game Spain had gone to Dublin with less pressure on their minds and beaten the Irish by 5-0.

The signs were not good when, only two weeks before the match in London, Meisl and Hogan watched their team struggle to beat a scratch Viennese side 2-1. The weather had been miserable, foggy and damp, which perfectly mirrored the outlook of both manager and trainer. Sindelar, the flimsy but

Jimmy Hogan during his time as manager
of Aston Villa (1936-1944).

This portrait of Hogan was taken in 1900, soon after he joined his first senior club, Nelson, as an eighteen-year-old.

(Above) The 22-year-old Hogan (middle row, second from the left) with his Burnley colleagues at the start of the 1905-06 season.
(Below) The family's time in Lausanne, where this picture was taken, became a treasured memory
(left to right: Jimmy, Joe, Frank, Evelyn, and Mary).

The MTK team that under Hogan won the 1926
Hungarian Cup Final, beating UTE 4-0.

Hogan leaps with joy as his protegé Richard Hofmann scores in Dresden Sports Club's 6-0 win over Guts Muts to win the championship of East Saxony in 1931.

Richard Hofmann, who took Hogan's advice and tuition to become one of Germany's most outstanding players, scoring twenty-four goals in twenty-five international appearances.

Perhaps the finest of Hogan's many discoveries, Gyorgy Orth, here only sixteen yet about to play for Hungary against Austria.

Rudi Hiden, the great "Wunderteam" goalkeeper of the 1930s, whom Hogan persuaded to join him at Racing Club de Paris.

Matthias Sindelar, frail yet brilliant centre forward of the "Wunderteam" that shocked England in 1932. A Jew, he died in strange circumstances in 1939.

(Right) Walter Nausch, the heart of the "Wunderteam". His close ball control was Hogan's idea of near perfection.

(Below) Hogan safe in Paris after escaping from Germany with his life savings sewn into those same Plus Fours.

(Above) The "Wunderteam" with their manager and close colleague of Hogan, Hugo Meisl. (Back row, left to right: Meisl, Luef, Jana, Gschweidl, Vogl, Hofmann, Sindelar, Nausch, Zischek; front row: Braun, Hiden, Sesztak.) (Below) Hogan instructs the Austrian team before their remarkable performance against England at Stamford Bridge in 1932.

(Above) Hogan at his desk while manager of Fulham in 1934.
(Below) He leaves hospital the following year having
recovered from appendicitis and, apparently, also from the
shock of being sacked while convalescing.

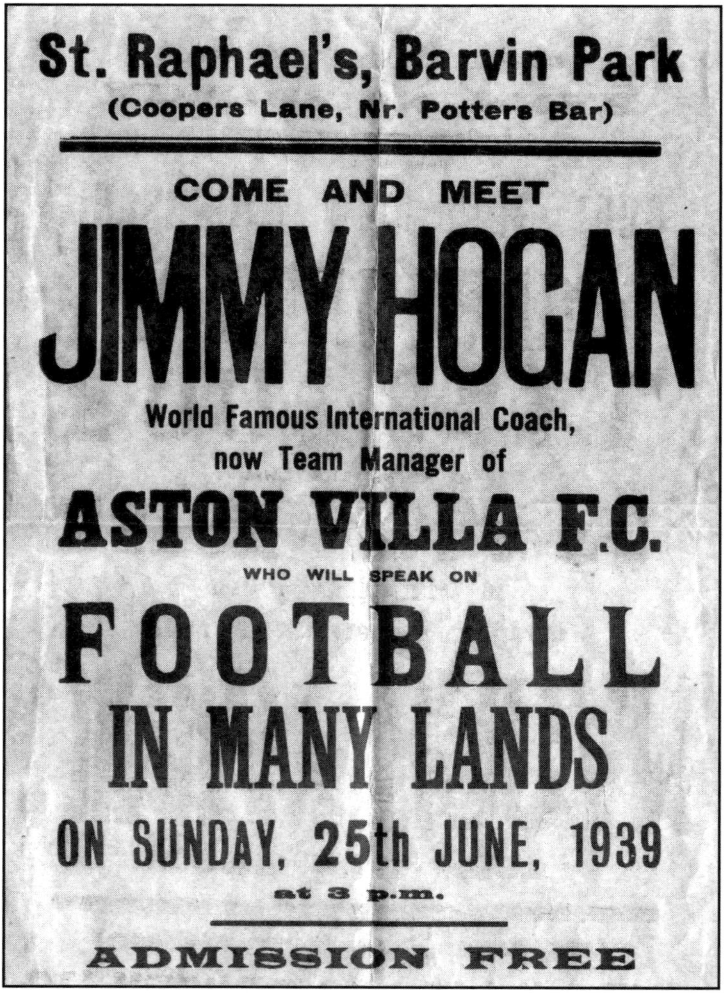


Advertising one of Hogan's lectures in 1939.

(Above) Hogan's relationship with Stanley Rous began badly but they worked together for the benefit of a new attitude towards coaching in England.
(Below) Hogan advises his class at the FA coaching course at the Duke of York's headquarters in 1936.

(Above) With the Aston Villa team he managed until the war stopped League football.

(Left) Hogan, still coaching in his seventies, with the Aston Villa manager and close friend Eric Houghton in 1954.

(Right) Sponsorship! Hogan accepted a national newspaper's invitation to coach youngsters. (Below) Schoolboys deep in concentration as Hogan gives a demonstration in 1947.

(Above) Still working with Aston Villa, many of these players were improved by his coaching. Among them was Peter McParland (second row, second player from the right), the outstanding Irish winger who was greatly influenced by Hogan. (Below) Students with the master. Hogan chats with Villa's star of the future, McParland (centre), and Ken O. Roberts, whose career was cut short by injury.

(Above) The match that finally proved Hogan right. Hungary score their fifth through Bozsik in 1953. Billy Wright (left) and Alf Ramsey (right) look on in dismay as Gil Merrick makes a forlorn attempt to stop Hungary's fifth goal against England in 1953.

(Below) Hogan (kneeling) with his highly successful Dresden Sports Club team, who were double champions of East Saxony and three times champions of Central Germany.

Few football men of his generation travelled
as far and wide as Hogan.

usually reliable goalscorer nicknamed 'Der Paperiener' (the Man of Paper), had been unwell and was in terrible form, regularly missing his scoring opportunities, usually with shots that went high over the crossbar. Yet undoubtedly he was the second most feared centre forward in Europe next to England's Bill (Dixie) Dean, which was strange since they were so different: one delicate and always relying on ball mastery in the Hogan manner while the other was awesomely powerful.

Back in Austria the fans had become less respectful to Meisl and Hogan. The pessimism was reflected in the Press. Journalists believed that the match in London would be "England against Rudi Hiden", who was still Austria's part-time goalkeeper (he was also a baker). But because he had earlier been denied the chance to play for Arsenal, Hiden had his own special reason for wanting to impress, as Hogan well knew.

It was not unusual for Meisl to take his worries into the public domain, but this time he seemed particularly depressed by fears of a deflating, heavy defeat. He was invited by a German newspaper to write a preview of the match and in it said it was a bad time to be meeting England. Austria, he admitted, were in poor form, had important players absent, especially forwards, and would probably succumb to England's physical buffeting. Hogan had often experienced Meisl's pessimistic outlook and tried to take no notice. In spite of the apparent lack of confidence, hundreds of fans went to Vienna railway station to give the team a supportive send-off.

Meisl instructed that dark suits should be issued to the players. Each member of the party was given a booklet explaining exactly how he should behave on the trip. On no account should he appear boastful. That particular instruction left Hogan concerned about confidence and he was in no hurry to discipline several of the players when they ignored it and began to say that given any luck and good weather they could beat England. Vogl, the left winger, even predicted a 2-0 victory. Sindelar suggested a narrow win for England.

The captain, Walter Nausch, who was later to become manager of the national side, was cautious, warning that the forwards would need to recover their form of several months earlier if they were to have any chance. Not that England were massively confident themselves. They had struggled to beat Ireland 1-0 and been held to a goalless draw by Wales. Controversially, the selectors decided to drop Dean and replace four other regular members of the forward line.

Upon the Austrian team's arrival in England it was Hogan who received the greatest attention from the Press. Pictures of him giving instructions to the team on a blackboard (see photo section) were shown in several papers. The story of his rise from Burnley player to become Europe's most respected international trainer seized the public's imagination, although there was also some criticism from people who believed he had sold his soul to the opposition.

A few days before the match he took the whole of the Austrian party to Stamford Bridge to see Chelsea play Everton, a game containing the two most eminent centre-forwards of the era, Everton's Dean and Hughie Gallacher, of Chelsea. Afterwards Hogan said he had not been impressed. According to him the fault was not that of the proven goalscorers but the coaches who had told defenders to hammer balls downfield in the hope of reaching them. Coaching at club level in England was in a sorry state. The Football Association was doing its best to encourage an upgrading of the system but at club level the advice was transparently being ignored.

The players in the England team, chosen by a remote and faceless FA selection committee, could hardly claim to be familiar with each other. Even so there were enough top class ones available to make it seem unlikely that the Austrians would depart with anything better than a two or three goal defeat. There was Harry Hibbs, one of the finest goalkeepers ever to play for England; David Jack, wonderfully gifted and the subject of the first £10,000 transfer (from Bolton to Arsenal); Billy Walker, of Aston Villa, who was captain, and his club partner, the goalscoring winger Eric Houghton, who became a close friend and later a colleague of Hogan. In defence, Roy Goodall and Ernie Blenkinsop formed the best partnership in the business. All in all, a good representation of English football of the time while Austria knew that Vogl and Gschweidl were suffering from minor injuries.

The teams were:

**England:** Hibbs (Birmingham), Goodall (Huddersfield Town), Blenkinsop (Sheffield Wednesday), Strange (Sheffield Wednesday), Hart (Leeds United), Keen (Derby County), Crooks (Derby County), Jack (Arsenal), Hampson (Blackpool), Walker (Aston Villa), Houghton (Aston Villa).
* It was originally intended that Tate would play at left half to form an Aston Villa grouping, but he had to withdraw with an injury.

**Austria:** Hiden; Rainer, Sesta, Nausch, Smistik, Gall, Zischek, Gschweidl, Sindelar, Schall, Vogl.

A crowd of about 42,000 turned up at Stamford Bridge, which was a disappointingly low attendance. Presumably the absentees assumed England would stroll to victory. So when England nearly scored within the first minute they probably felt justified in not bothering to turn up. In Vienna officials and fans listening on the "wireless" came to the early but premature conclusion that they were about to witness a rout. Jack went out to the right, took possession and sent the ball across goal but Houghton missed it. The mistake was quickly overcome.

# PROPHET OR TRAITOR?

England went ahead with a goal that emphasised exactly what Hogan had warned the Austrians. Some of the England players were still suffering from coaching based on the "get rid of it" philosophy but they were not all without natural, deceptive ball control and positive finishing ability. Hibbs cleared. Hart played a long ball. Jack and Hampson exchanged neat, precise passes under pressure. Hampson ran on and beat the nervous Hiden with a low shot. Indeed, the whole Austrian side looked worried.

Back in Austria the listeners convinced themselves that their team would soon be floundering, but Meisl and Hogan had worked hard on the side's preparation to ensure that the defence could retreat quickly and start counter-attacks that left the opposition struggling to get back into shape. Gradually their tuition began to reap rewards. It became obvious that the Austrians were the more skillful side but after twenty-six minutes Hampson scored again. However, Sindelar and Smistik became more and more involved, particularly in those moments when Zischek (known as the "Ghost") caused the England defence all sorts of problems as he weaved elusive patterns along the right wing. Vogl missed a clear chance in front of Hibbs and Hiden, gaining confidence, pulled off an astonishing save to tip the ball over the crossbar from Houghton. The Austrians used their individual deftness but also carefully defined long passes to disturb England. Hogan's trademarks were written all over their tactics but at half-time he and Meisl had to tell their players to stop giving the English players so much respect.

Although early in the second half Hiden cleverly deflected a shot from Houghton over the bar, Austria showed England that they had plenty to worry about. Sindelar played a typically accurate ball to Schall, who in turn swept it square to Zischek and he thrust it beyond Hibbs. Suddenly England were in more trouble than they had ever experienced against foreign opposition on home ground. They were forced to

116

defend almost on their own goalline. Four corners had to be beaten out. Nausch's header hit a post and Hibbs somehow blocked a robust drive from Schall. The crowd generously warmed to the opposition, applauding their moves and attempts on goal.

England pulled themselves together. Hiden had to make last-second saves from Jack and Houghton and was unlucky to concede a third goal when Houghton hit a powerful free-kick which flew towards the line of defenders. Schall elected to duck, presumably hoping that Hiden had the shot covered, but the ball still hit his head and went past the wrong-footed goalkeeper. At 3-1 England ought to have had control. Far from it. By then it was obvious that they were inferior in many respects, not least in subtlety.

Deservedly, Austria retrieved a goal. Again Sindelar's superb control was the essential ingredient. Not far into the England half, he received the ball from Vogl and ran on past a couple of ill-timed tackles. Closing in on goal and remembering Hogan's lectures about making "time and space", he seemed to have all the time he needed to control the situation and tease Hibbs before placing his shot in the net to make the score 3-2. Even the Belgian referee, John Langenus, could not help commenting after the match: "Sindelar's goal was a masterpiece which no one ever again accomplished against such opponents as the English. Not before him, not after him." Yet if England's teamwork was inferior, they still had enough individually proficient players to avoid the potential terrible embarrassment of a defeat. Walker laid the ball off to the Derby County winger Sammy Crooks who unexpectedly tried a long-range shot which surprised Hiden and beat him. Austria kept coming back. Five minutes from the end Hibbs found himself blocked in trying to move off the goal line to intercept a corner and Zischek comfortably turned in Austria's third goal (4-3).

# PROPHET OR TRAITOR?

Although England seemed to make the score a more respectable 5-3, their final attempt was disallowed, the whistle having already gone. Walker claimed that if the teams met again England would score at least eight goals. Some critics belittled the Austrian achievement, claiming that their football was not as original as some writers had suggested. Yet most critics acclaimed the performance, particularly pointing out that the Austrians had shown what could be achieved if real skill was linked to pace. It was widely agreed that had their finishing been as effective as their approach work they would have inflicted upon England their first home defeat.

Hugo Meisl's younger brother Willy, who after the Second World War wrote enlightened articles in the British magazine World Sports, recalled an experience that, for him, epitomised the reactions of the public to the Austrian performance. "A few years later when I had moved to England I went again to Stamford Bridge. A ticket was supposed to have been deposited for me with the giant commissionaire. I asked him rather shyly: 'Do you have an envelope for Meisl?' He began to look through his biggish pile of envelopes and I grew uncertain whether he had understood my pronunciation of my foreign name, or whether perhaps the ticket had not been deposited for me at all. So I started spelling Meisl just when the man found the envelope. He handed it to me with the self-assurance of a sergeant-major, which he most probably had been. Calmly and with sincerity he said: 'I shall never forget this name as long as I live'. It certainly was one of the finest compliments ever paid to Hugo and his so-called 'Wunderteam'."

The English Press, which over many years had rarely given praise to Continental sides, had to admit that the match against Austria was an eminent moment in the game's history. Hogan had to be given credit not only for his work with this Austrian team but in the years before. The Daily Herald's report by

# HIS GREATEST HONOUR

"Corinthian" began: "A most disturbing victory - the kind that leaves one wondering how it happened and a sort of creepy feeling that we were successful by the kindness of some spirit of chance that will never be so good again."

The writer conceded: "Definitely and beyond all shadow of doubt, Austria played football better than England did." He pointed out: "In style of play, such as making passes along the ground so that the receiver should be able to make good use of the ball quickly, in getting to open spaces to make a pass possible and even in control of the ball and in every sense, the Austrian forwards and half-backs were better than ours." He summed up the experience by saying: "Never before has any Continental team succeeded in making England's best defence look anxious, compelling them to take hasty kicks which meant slicing the ball to all sorts of useless positions.

"It was the brilliance of these Austrian forwards that occasioned this shakiness among our defenders. The visitors did not possess a forward who was weak, but England did. Individually - I must insist upon dealing with the better team first - the Austrians were also superior. Sindelar is the best centre-forward the Continent has ever sent to England. I cannot remember a move, a touch, or feint, or a pass which was made by him unless it was to the advantage of his side. Schall, the inside-left, was a schemer of the highest class." In other words, the Austrians carried out everything Meisl and Hogan had encouraged, and Sindelar had come to his peak in the country of Hogan's birth.

Recognition of Sindelar's ability was well deserved. His willowy physique and his ability to glide and swerve past defenders made him almost impossible to mark. With some notable exceptions, his goalscoring was not all that it might have been but he made opportunities for others. He said that Hogan's "shrewd judgement" had meant everything to the team when they played England. "He said to us in the dressing room a minute or two before the kick-off: 'Now remember even if this is the hub of sport, the game is just football as you have played it before.'"

His own life had parallels with that of Hogan. His father had moved from his home country (in Sindelar's case it was Moravia, which became the Czech Republic) to Vienna to seek work as a mason. The family settled in an industrial area of the city and Matthias developed his football talents with a home-made ball of rags. His ability to dribble with it completely mystified his friends, just as Hogan had so impressed his own school-mates.

The Sindelar family had never been well off and their situation was made far worse when Matthias's father was killed in action in the third year of the First World War. Though only fourteen, Matthias had to take work as a mechanic but also played for Herthan in the town of Favoriten. He later joined "Amateure", the club that was to be re-formed as the famous FK Austria. Fair-haired, over six feet in height and slight, he looked far too frail to think of a career as a professional player. He suffered several injuries and at one point, in another mirror image of Hogan's early days, he had a serious knee problem that required surgery. He also suffered badly from "growing pains" in the joints.

His elusive style and aesthetic face may have brought about that nickname suggesting frailty (Der Papleriener) but he was never afraid to risk a 50-50 tackle. His fitness was such that he could go back to break up an attack and then take the ball more than half the length of the pitch, avoid defenders and finish much more powerfully than his appearance would suggest. He was one of the outstanding players in the early days of the Mitropa Cup, which was the precursor of the European Cup and was first devised by Meisl in 1927. Many of the central European countries took part in the original competition and Sindelar later led FK Austria to two victories in finals.

# HIS GREATEST HONOUR

Following Sindelar's appearance in England, several British clubs desperately wanted to persuade him to stay. The Austrian FA would have none of it. He remained a prominent member of the national side but in the 1934 World Cup he was literally kicked into submission by the Italians who went on to become world champions. By the time Austria qualified for the 1938 World Cup in Paris their country was occupied by the Germans so they were unable to go to France. The Jewish clubs were closed down and their players ostracised, yet in spite of his own Jewish background Sindelar remained captain when the national team was renamed by the Germans "Ostmark". He even played on the occasion in 1938 when they met Germany in a match supposed to "celebrate" Germany's taking over of Austria. He demanded that his team wore Austria's traditional red and white. They won 2-0 and he scored a fine, defiant goal.

He, like several other members of the old Austrian national side, was ordered to play in the "Greater German" team for the World Cup finals. He was appalled at the idea and made the excuses that at thirty-five he was too old and had too many injuries. Yet still the Germans knew that he was one of the best players in the world. Their coach, Sepp Herberger, was either unaware of Sindelar's Jewish background or chose to ignore it. He said: "He was revered in soccer circles. He asked me politely to leave him out. When I insisted again and again, I got the impression that there were other reasons for him to refuse. I almost had the impression that it was dismay and hostility at the political developments which weighed on him and was the reason for him to refuse. Finally I gave up. I thought I understood him. He looked as if a heavy burden had been taken off his shoulders when I told him."

Sindelar was in mental turmoil. His club had been disbanded and so, too, he believed, had Austria itself. Colleagues got out of the country but he remained, living with

# PROPHET OR TRAITOR?

his mother in a modest ground-floor apartment helping her in the running of a laundry. He also owned a coffee house. His good looks and quiet, modest character made him highly popular with women yet he never seemed to have a lasting relationship. On January 23, 1939 he was found dead next to an unconscious Italian woman, Camilia Castagnola, who never recovered. Although it was suggested that she was a regular girlfriend, seemingly he had known her for only a few days. The post-mortem gave "carbon monoxide poisoning" as the cause of both deaths and there was talk of a defective flue in the apartment. Naturally, there were rumours of suicide and stories that he was in fear of his life from the Nazis. The rumours turned to legend. Every year on the anniversary of his death players and officials past and present go to the Central Cemetery in Vienna to pay respects to Austria's greatest ever player.

Hogan was shocked to hear of Sindelar's death. He was aware of the stories that another member of the Austrian national team, who was a fanatical follower of the Nazi party, informed the Gestapo that Sindelar was a Jew. There is little doubt that Sindelar was in danger of future persecution and there were even suggestions that he had been murdered, but whether or not his fear led to his ending his own life in a gas-filled room or if the historic irony of that possibility was all too appealing to a succession of post-war writers and even poets, it is impossible to say.

Austria's magnificent performance in London was further enhanced when in 1936 England went to Vienna and lost 2-1. Yet still English football attempted to ignore the rise of the Continent. Scotland, whose players had provided Hogan with the incentive to produce intelligent teams, were similarly guilty. Although they had played abroad before, their first official international match against Continental opposition had been against France in Paris in 1930 and resulted in a 2-0 win plus some substantial financial rewards for their visit. That encouraged them to make another tour in the following summer. They chose Austria, Italy and Switzerland. The players were expecting a pleasant, easy close-season trip with no serious competition. They had underestimated the work that Hogan, and others, had been doing. In Vienna they were totally outplayed, and even out-run, by the Austrians and lost 5-0. The result was read in disbelief back home in Scotland. They went on to Rome and lost 3-0 to Italy. Even Switzerland were beaten by only 3-2.

In the hope of gaining vengeance and retrieving their prestige, in 1933 the Scottish FA invited Austria to play in Glasgow. The Austrians became the first national team to visit Scotland. In spite of what had happened at Stamford Bridge, it was widely assumed that the atmosphere would be so oppressive for the visitors that Scotland would have a comfortable victory. Far from it. They were lucky to draw 2-2.

In spite of the doubts expressed ahead of their visit to London there was no question that in the early Thirties the Austrians were at the pinnacle of their form, which in a way was a pity since they did not have the opportunity to prove the point in the World Cup. By the 1934 finals they were in decline. Once again England had refused to compete and the British Press virtually ignored the whole tournament. Austria struggled to beat an ordinary French side by 3-2 after extra-time in the first round but defeated Hungary 2-1 in the second. That brought them up against Italy in the semi-finals, which was a great disappointment to the crowds and the organisers since it had always been hoped that these two would meet in the final. Italy, guided by the wise Pozzo, won 1-0 on a heavy pitch which did not suit the Austrians, and within a few months the side broke up.

# 12

# Frustration at Fulham

HIS WORK WITH AUSTRIA complete, Hogan returned to Britain without a job. However, in May, 1934 he was approached by Fulham with whom he had originally been motivated to think of a career in coaching. He joined them for one not particularly happy season as manager-coach. The club had been managed by James MacIntyre who had been under the impression that he could turn himself into a version of Herbert Chapman, British football's first truly powerful and influential manager. By frequent use of the transfer market MacIntyre took Fulham out of the Third Division. In the 1932-33 season he had organised a good run in the Second Division, only for the team to falter over the last few games and miss promotion. In the following season the ambitions of the club waned and in a desperate attempt at revival MacIntyre sold the successful striker Frank Newton to Reading and bought Arsenal's Jack Lambert, who was clearly over the hill. The team continued to decline and in February, 1934 MacIntyre was finally dismissed, never to obtain another job in the game.

Hogan, now fifty-two, immediately won the appreciation of the fans, astutely and diplomatically re-signing Newton from Reading. In the Fulham handbook for the 1934-35 season, he introduced himself to the fans with this painfully ingratiating essay: "After spending a score of years in exile, teaching the foreigner how to play, I now make my bow as manager-coach to my dear old club. Can you imagine how honoured and delighted I feel? Despite the fact that I had a wonderful time abroad, and coached the international teams of different countries on at least fifty occasions, there has been an eternal longing in my breast. I have often found myself humming those old music hall songs: "Homeland! Homeland! When shall I see thee again", and "Take me back to London Town". As far as the Continent is concerned, the day-dreams of my youth have been fulfilled. I have sailed in the Mediterranean, climbed the Swiss Alps, bathed in the blue Danube, saw the wonderful cities of Vienna, Budapest, Berlin, Rome, Amsterdam, Zurich, Stockholm etc and obtained a slight knowledge of various languages. All wonderful in a way. But what a treat it is to see the English countryside again! How wonderful to spend a pleasant weekend in the Valley of the Thames." If that was his romantic conception of what life was to be like back home, he was quickly disabused.

His playing staff included his son Joe who must have had mixed feelings, proud that his father's attitude to coaching was still so strong that it had barely changed from the days when he first moved to the Continent but worried about the reception he might receive. The question was whether those deeply held beliefs would convince the more experienced members of the staff. Incredibly, training in England still remained based on large amounts of time being devoted to maintaining fitness and little with the ball. He changed all that but the directors were unhappy. He said that he was working hard and constructively, teaching his "on-the-carpet" football as he always had. He still had no love of the withdrawn centre half tactic which had been adopted throughout the country, but it was his constant emphasis on a possession game and individual skills that many of the players failed to have in their natural repertoire that again caused problems.

# PROPHET OR TRAITOR?

His own seemingly never-waning ability to do things with a ball that many of those he was instructing would probably never be able to achieve themselves won over some players but caused resentment in others. That, in turn, cost the team as a whole their confidence. Once the senior players turned against him things got worse (shades of Chelsea in the Gianluca Vialli era when many contemporary commentators seemed to believe that player-power was something new).

He had been in charge for only thirty-one matches when he was taken ill and rushed to hospital for an appendicitis operation. Heartlessly, it was while there recovering after complications had set in that the club sacked him. The excuse was that the senior players were not in need of coaching. "When I became convalescent," he said, "I received the shock of my life." The club sent a director to the hospital with a statement confirming the decision to end his contract. "I was just pushed aside with no salary," he said. "I took the matter to the FA and it was dealt with in a few minutes - and the verdict was in my favour." Fulham agreed that he had been unfairly dismissed. Even so, he was grievously disappointed that his first attempt to establish himself as a manager in Britain after so many successful years abroad had come to such an end.

His sacking was not even mentioned in Fulham's programme for the match after the event. He was even more frustrated because he had been hoping to sign Jackie Gibbons who later became manager of Brentford but at the time was an excitingly promising player. While Hogan was in hospital Gibbons was advised to give up his playing career and to join the RAF.

The only satisfactory outcome of the Fulham experience was that it put Hogan in contact with the new FA Secretary, Stanley Rous, who in spite of some difficult setbacks in their relationship became something of an ally and fellow believer in the value of coaching. Hogan appealed to him to obtain compensation from Fulham. That was not within the jurisdiction of the FA but Rous said he had always felt that it was the duty of the association to help all footballers, managers and coaches. He contacted Fulham and asked them to consider whether or not they felt that they had treated Hogan fairly. They agreed to make a payment. In no way would Rous and Hogan ever become close, but Hogan later gave him credit for being one of the few people in Britain who consistently warned that without a complete change in outlook towards the importance of coaching, Continental football would sooner rather than later overtake that of the Football League clubs and subsequently the national side.

He was thoroughly disillusioned by his whole experience at Fulham and vowed to go back to the Continent where he would be appreciated. Meanwhile, at Craven Cottage the club relied disproportionately on one player, Joe Edelston, whom Hogan had encouraged to take up coaching, which he did. Edelston stayed with the club for seventeen years and loyally often acted as temporary manager, but in the end Fulham again used the excuse that senior players did not need coaching and sacked him. His son, Maurice, played for the club and later became a much-respected commentator with the BBC.

Always stout in his own defence, Hogan said of his dismissal: "As my character was of the best and I was a conscientious workman in the bargain, I can only come to one conclusion, that I was sacked for teaching my ideas of football played in an intelligent manner." But he was rarely out of work for long and soon after leaving Fulham he at last received some recognition from the FA. One of their officials showed him the proposed script of a film about young players. He liked it and went to New Malden to help with the filming of schoolboy football. Among the youngsters who impressed him was Reg Lewis. "I formed a great opinion of him," he said "and resolved to hand my discovery over to George Allison, the manager of Arsenal. He told Allison that, given the chance, Lewis would not only play for Arsenal but also for England, which he did. Lewis scored both goals for the club when they beat Liverpool 2-0 in the 1950 Cup Final.

The FA's decision to make a film about young players was in large measure spurred by the comments that Herbert Chapman had made about the need for better and more extensive coaching of youngsters. Arsenal had sponsored a scheme which Chapman said had "enormous possibilities". However, he had warned: "Unless its scope is extended, a golden opportunity will be missed." He had said it should be expanded across the whole country, giving "working class youths" everywhere the opportunity to receive professional coaching. He added that the FA should distribute a coaching film throughout the country and open a football school. He concluded: "I shall consider the scheme has failed unless the FA can be persuaded to further coaching on a grand scale, catering for every class of player." Hence, the FA's call to Hogan to assist in the making of the subsequent film.

Wherever he worked he always made sure that there was a clause in his contract making it clear that if the Austrian federation ever wanted him to return he could do so without penalty. As a result when Meisl heard that he had fallen out with Fulham he got in touch. So Europe's most effective partnership re-formed. They shared the coaching of the national team and Hogan was asked to search the country for good amateurs to make ready for the 1936 Olympic Games in Berlin. In spite of being middle-aged, his appetite for football and coaching was undiminished and the esteem in which he was held in Austria was shown by the fact that he was called upon to be trainer to their national team against England (twice), Scotland, Spain, Italy, Portugal and France.

As for the Olympics, the group of players he gathered together seemed inadequate and ill-prepared. He said: "It was pathetic when I first took them over. Most of these fellows earn as little as from ten shillings to seventeen and sixpence a week, owing to the economic situation, and can scarcely afford the bare necessities of life. First I had to treat their bodies, then their minds. We went to Salzburg for special preparation, good food and plenty of it. It was so strange that it bowled them over. I feared the worst but once I had set them up physically, treating the mind was an easy matter."

A typical reaction to the news that his immense coaching talent had again been lost to the country of his birth was that of the Sunday Dispatch correspondent John Robertson who wrote: "Silver-haired James Hogan, prince of coaches, left England yesterday to coach the Austrian team for the Olympic Games. It is a crying shame. England has need of his genius for demonstrating soccer. It would be a wonderful gesture if the FA kept him here, gave him £1,000 a year, put him in charge of all our representative teams, and let him organise the coaching scheme in the schools."

Robertson also said: "We are sending a team to the Olympic Games. Hogan will be coaching one of the opposing teams, although he would be much happier looking after the British players. For twenty years he has been our greatest sporting ambassador - he speaks four or five languages - but his heart is still with England, and if we are to compete against the modern Continental methods he is the man to get the best results." Hogan himself had said that he thought the British team would probably be eliminated after the first round, but he did point out that at least they were genuinely amateur. He was proved right.

Before the Olympic Games Austria's national side under the dual control of Hogan and Meisl beat England 2-1 in Vienna. This must have been immensely satisfying for Meisl following the undeserved defeat at Stamford Bridge, but another of those days of disturbingly divided loyalty for

# PROPHET OR TRAITOR?

Hogan. The victory was all the more gratifying because the England side was formed on a nucleus of the fine Arsenal team of the time. Yet the six players chosen from Highbury had been involved in a strenuous programme of three matches within seven days.

Meisl thought that the Arsenal players would probably find the second half hard going. Hogan, knowing full well that fitness amongst English players was always the least of their problems, was less convinced and mentioned that two or three of the side Meisl had selected were not ideal if the game became a battle of stamina over wits. Meisl said he was not concerned about that because he was convinced that the match would be won by his team within the first twenty minutes. He was quoted as saying: "We shall score two or three goals and then we shall be forced to defend."

The prediction was justified. Austria duly scored two goals in the first twenty minutes. England were forced to defend and had not more than half a dozen opportunities to break out with any chance of scoring themselves. The weather was oppressively warm yet Sindelar's pace never faltered. He continually made space in the approaches to the England penalty area and the experienced Arsenal defenders Eddie Hapgood and George Male were constantly under pressure. In the end Austria became weary, leaving George Camsell to score in the tenth minute of the second half. Meisl was desperate to see Austria retain their lead, even going to sit behind their goal as if to look the English forwards in the eyes and will them not to score. Then, as his team counter-attacked, he ran to the touchline, his bowler hat falling to the ground, and seemed to be offering himself as an extra winger. He had no need to worry. Austria held on and the Meisl-Hogan partnership had its laurels.

Reflecting on the many fascinating and exciting matches he saw, Hogan would always mention that game against England but said that Austria's 5-4 victory over Spain in Madrid was the single most stirring game he ever witnessed. It also brought him a reminder that an "artificial stimulant", as we would now call alcohol, was then accepted as the normal half-time pick-me-up and, when offered by the home side, was often over-generous. He went into the dressing room before the game and saw a dozen bottles of beer and one of brandy on a table and realised that if his team got through it all they would almost inevitably have lost concentration (not to speak of balance) in the second half. He demanded that it was all removed, apart from the brandy. "I put that in my pocket until the match was won." However, it was a visit to Rome for a meeting with Italy that put such small dramas into the shade.

The dictator Mussolini was the centre of attention. The Italian players knew that if they failed to win they would be in trouble. They kicked the Austrians unmercifully and left them with only nine men. However, the game finished 2-2, which smacked of political correctness but was far from what Mussolini had demanded. Austria's Prince Starhemberg had been with Mussolini in the VIP seats and afterwards went down to the pitch to congratulate the players and Hogan, whom he called "Shimmy". Mussolini stormed out, leaving the Italian players shaking with fear. Hogan spent the train journey back to Vienna treating his own men for their injuries.

Progress in building the Olympic team went well until the president of the Austrian FA told the players that they had been paid a "great compliment" by the English FA, who had asked him if they could spare Hogan to go back to England as "Chief Instructor" on the first FA coaching course in 1936. The Austrians said that they were so honoured that they had even insisted on paying his expenses. The "Chief Instructor" title was a slight exaggeration since there were several other instructors who were all given much the same standing but at last the FA had bowed, slightly, to pressure to reap some of Hogan's talent.

# PROPHET OR TRAITOR?

Versions of what happened at the first course vary. According to Hogan, he had about one hundred "pupils" including such talents as Wilf Copping, Alex James, Frank Moss, Frank Barson, Arthur Rowe, Eric Houghton, Joe Mercer, Peter Doherty and Billy Walker as well as leading managers, among them George Allison (Arsenal) and Stan Seymour (Newcastle United) together with Arsenal's trainer Tom Whittaker.

His version of events was that at the end of the day he was cheered and that Allison in particular was greatly impressed by his lecture and demonstration, even asking him whether he would join the Arsenal staff when he finished working with the Austrians. Nothing ever came of that, although he did have lengthy discussions at Highbury before turning down the offer.

Rous, later to become Sir Stanley, distinguished president of FIFA, told a different story. To his lasting credit, he realised that his own experience as a schoolmaster had shown that little was being done in England in the way of training for young players, let alone the professionals, and that facilities were poor. He worked to improve the situation, setting up knock-out competitions for juniors and a County Youth Championship. He was equally concerned about the standard of coaching at the senior level which was why he decided to start training courses for coaches and referees. The question of who coaches the coaches is one that has never had a convincing answer.

Rous's ambition was to have professional coaches develop the game at all levels, including amateur - a revolutionary thought in those days. There had been long-standing and bitter criticism of the whole idea of leading players and coaches actually needing such instruction and Rous confessed that the first course was not as successful as he had anticipated. He claimed that none of the lecturers "proved expert" in putting over their subjects. In fact he maintained that more than anything the original course proved that the instructors needed instruction themselves. But he did say that although he was annoyed that Hogan was unwilling to submit advance notes of his session "in case too much might be learnt about his methods", he was "the most forceful and interesting".

Rous came to the conclusion that Hogan was not seriously interested in "passing on the best in coaching methods". Mysteriously, he said he was alarmed that Hogan was ill-organised as far as taking practical periods were concerned. He thought that practical coaching should have been the area in which Hogan had advantages over the other coaches. He had made it clear that because the course was a short, introductory version of what might develop into longer sessions at a later date, each period had to run to time. He was furious that for his forty-five minute session Hogan "wasted" five minutes taking his group to the most remote part of the field and then had to ask someone to return because he had forgotten to take any footballs with him. This seems curious since it would have been the first time in Hogan's career that he failed to ensure that there were almost as many footballs as players to coach (see photo section).

According to Rous's account he implored Hogan to suggest some exercises while the group waited for the footballs. Hogan, so Rous said, was reluctant. Either way, the balls arrived. Hogan got one and talked and demonstrated for far longer than Rous had planned. In the end there was insufficient time for the group to carry out any exercises. Rous also criticised Hogan for standing with his back to a strong sun which shone directly at the class, forcing its members to shield their eyes in order to see his demonstration, which, typically, included a dozen ways to trap the ball with the inside or outside of either foot, with the toe, heel, instep, chest and head. Impressive though the demonstration was, Rous said it was done too quickly for the class to assimilate its content and it was too advanced for a class only wanting to know how to bring the ball under control as quickly as possible. That, again, seemed a strange thing to say since the majority of those on the course were already senior professionals.

Apart from criticising Hogan's coaching ability on the course, Rous disingenuously also cast doubts on his reputation abroad which, in spite of his earlier compliment, he suggested was "in part fortuitous". He said that the core of Hogan's work on the Continent amounted to "endless demonstrations of his own high skills". He said that Hogan would put up a board with a hole in the middle barely larger than a football. From fifteen yards he would slot eight shots out of ten into the hole, which Rous concluded was his favourite "trick". Far from being a trick, the success rate came about as a result of years of practice and in all of that time it had never before failed to be greeted with amazement. Clearly the English football establishment's deep mistrust of individuality, special skill and a touch of arrogance was as deep as ever, sadly not excluding Rous himself.

Reiterating his attempts to play down Hogan's achievements on the Continent, Rous suggested that because he "could not speak the Austrian players' own language" (which was very much a former schoolmaster's attitude to anyone who was not word perfect), he had to rely on the demonstrations. Without any personal experience of seeing Hogan at work abroad, Rous was prepared to suggest that the Austrians had soon become disillusioned and bored when they rarely got a single ball through the hole in a board. He maintained that in Austria Meisl had to intervene to persuade the players not to give up but continue practising until they could get near to emulating Hogan. Even so, Rous admitted that the Austrians became "an effective team". Yet at the conclusion of the FA course he said Hogan had "made it clear that on his own he lacked many of the organisational skills a coach requires". Nobody had the courage to mention Stamford

# FRUSTRATION AT FULHAM

Bridge, 1932 or any of the other achievements that had revolutionised Continental football.

The opinions of others on the course, or those who were invited observers, were much different. The journalist Ivan Sharpe, writing in The Sunday Chronicle, said he was immediately impressed as Hogan explained to sixty "students" how he had watched Alex James perform a swerve in an Arsenal match, noted it and practised it until he could do exactly the same. Hogan demonstrated it in front of "wee Alec" himself. Sharpe concluded that Hogan had shown that although he was considered to be the world's greatest coach, he could still learn from the current stars of the game.

James himself was won over. He said that the course persuaded him that coaching was not after all "moonshine". He added: "As a rule footballers are born, but after watching Jimmy Hogan I was convinced that they can also be made. Even at his age he has perfect ball control, and, what is even more surprising, the ability to make every movement look simple even to the novice - and few of us taking the course could be described as novices. I feel certain that his methods would improve the mobility of our young players, make them think more quickly, and place skill above mere speed and bustle."

Hogan often mentioned to his "pupils" that James was a perfect example of a player who could control the ball and feint all in one movement, but when he asked the great Scottish international to show how it was done he failed on half a dozen occasions even to control the ball. George Allison put it down to James not really understanding what he did so naturally on the field in match situations.

Sharpe had seen Hogan's demonstrations more than ten years earlier but said that the essence of his coaching was unchanged. This was, he said, a coach who never said: "Do as I say, not as I do". He could still do everything he preached.

135

# PROPHET OR TRAITOR?

"He is brilliantly expert in all he demonstrates - ball control, swerving, heading and all the rest of it. A marvel."

Allison took seven members of his coaching and playing staff to the course and recalled that in the lunch break instead of resting, Hogan took on the Danish international Nils Middelboe at tennis. Middelboe, who played for Chelsea, was a formidable six footer and considerable tennis player, but Hogan beat him.

In spite of his criticism, Rous was not so put off as to omit Hogan from the second FA course which was held at the Chelsea barracks playing fields. This time the session, which was residential and held over a week, was even better attended, particularly by senior players. Rous insisted on the pooling of ideas and methods. Among the instructors was Walter Winterbottom, who was to became England's first national team manager. Hogan was invited to teach tactics but this time Rous insisted that he was accompanied by a tutor who was supposed to create a link between the coach, the demonstrator and the "pupils". The course was acknowledged as a success, even by those who had previously been doubtful about the need for its existence. Rous himself felt that it would greatly improve the teaching of football at schools and stop the growing drift towards rugby.

In spite of his reservations when, many years later, Rous heard of Hogan's death, he graciously wrote to the family acknowledging the contribution he had made to international football.

Among the players who were most impressed with the second coaching session was Joe Mercer, then the Arsenal captain and later to become a highly respected manager (including, briefly and refreshingly being in charge of England). After England had lost to Hungary at Wembley in 1953 he wrote to Hogan saying: "I look back very often to the FA Instructional Classes and feel very sure that those basic fundamental principles, which you so cleverly used to put over to us, have been responsible for whatever success I may have achieved." One of the finest of Irish internationals, Peter Doherty, also wrote to say: "Heartiest congratulations. Remember I was one of your youngsters once and I haven't done so badly."

# 13

# Olympic Farce

THE COACHING WORK FOR the FA was a mere interlude. When he got back to link up with the Austrian Olympic team he began to realise that the Games of 1936 would be as much a battle between ideologies as a sports competition. These were to become the most controversial Olympics in history. Adolf Hitler had said that the Olympic movement helped "strengthen the bonds of peace between the nations" and promptly and cynically used the Games to further the idea of a world-dominating Germany. But while his walk-out after seeing the black American Jesse Owens win the long jump was the most obvious sign of his displeasure, the football competition also concentrated attention on his inability to contemplate a German defeat in any field.

Hogan faced a much different situation to anything he had experienced during previous periods in Austria. This time the players who had been brought together to be shaped into a team capable of winning the gold medal were not experienced professionals but a group of amateurs, many of whom played for modest Austrian sides. In a way he found that easier than working with men with preconceived ideas. The younger ones, particularly, were, as with many before them and many more to come, captivated by his ability to do anything he asked them to do, but better. Once again any problems with communication were overcome by his exhibitions.

# OLYMPIC FARCE

The Germans had been preparing their team for months and with far more players at their training camp than should have been allowed under the Olympic rules. However, many other countries were also unashamedly nationalistic in their belief that a successful Olympic team would do much in terms of international prestige. Several countries had employed well-known players as coaches, among them Poland who called in Alex James. Meanwhile, Britain had not even decided to send a team until early July - the Games were due to begin on August 1. The Great Britain players were selected only two weeks before they were to leave for Germany - such was the attitude of the officials to proper preparation. Fortunately Rous, personally, had suggested to several of the leading amateurs that they remained in training during the summer. The training consisted of meeting twice a week at the Fulham ground and being coached by Joe Edelston and Bill Voisey.

When Hogan arrived in Berlin with his Austrian team he, like everyone else, was amazed to find a 100,000 capacity, all-seated stadium and a huge Olympic village. Training facilities for all of the competitors were far better than ever seen in previous Games. Ominously, though, the map of the village given to the visiting team officials showed that the whole site was in the shape of Germany with the German competitors housed in an overflow section which, on the map, corresponded to the area of Czechoslovakia which later Germany would annex.

In spite of the growing reputation of the Austrians under Hogan's guidance, Great Britain were made joint favourites with Germany. Presumably this was based on past Olympic history, but it had been back in 1908 and 1912 when Britain last won the football competition. One of the British players was Bernard Joy, of Arsenal, who became the authoritative Football Correspondent of the Evening Standard. He said that

139

# PROPHET OR TRAITOR?

he found it amazing that many of his colleagues happily accepted Britain's unrealistic placing as a favourite simply because they still held the belief that Continental football was far inferior. All that the organisers had done was to select what they considered were the eight strongest countries and the eight weakest and paired them off in the first round. But the idea did not go entirely to plan. Japan, making their first appearance, beat Sweden 3-2, although they were then beaten 8-0 by Italy.

Germany thrashed Luxembourg 9-0 in the first round while Austria got off to a quiet start, beating Egypt 3-1. China then made the football of the British team look ugly but still lost 2-0. Poland, well prepared, totally outclassed Britain and at one point were leading 5-1, eventually winning 5-4. But the big surprise of the second round was a 2-0 win for Norway over Germany. Some members of the British team later went round to the German quarters to offer a little sporting consolation, only to find that Hitler, who had been watching the game, had left a message telling the whole team to disband and go home.

Hogan then became immersed in the biggest controversy of the tournament. With ten minutes remaining of Austria's second round match against Peru, they were 4-2 down. One of his team was injured and had to leave the field, returning in a few minutes. The Peruvians claimed that it was not the same player. Hogan was embroiled in a touchline struggle involving players of both sides and several hundred spectators who had come on to the pitch. The spectators began to lash out, mainly at the Austrians. A German referee who had been sitting in the grandstand went on to the pitch and threw himself at a spectator who was about to punch one of the Austrian players. It was mayhem and there was no way the match could continue. Later a five-man jury concluded that the game would have to be replayed behind closed doors but the Peruvians refused to be involved, were disqualified and returned home. Had they stayed they may well have won the final.

# OLYMPIC FARCE

The semi-final brought Austria up against Poland. Surprisingly, Austria won more comfortably than even they thought likely, by 3-1, and at the end all of the team ran to the touchline to embrace Hogan who had done his homework on the Poles in their earlier matches. In the meantime Pozzo guided his Italian team of "amateurs", who in reality were mostly young professionals, to the final, which would be as much about the two best coaches in the world as the teams they led. Italy's left winger, Gabrotti, took them into the lead during the second half but Austria's centre forward Steinmetz equalised. The match went into extra-time. In the early minutes Austria's outside right, Frossi, who wore spectacles and needed to have a band around his forehead to stop the sweat clouding them, decided to retreat into the middle of a crowded goalmouth and help his defence. He misjudged an interception. Hogan had to accept the incongruity of Italy's winning goal coming not from any skillful moment of artistry, of which he would have approved, but from a simple rebound off Frossi's shins. Overall, though, he felt justified in his much earlier remarks that Italy would become a serious force in world football.

A year later Austria were re-establishing themselves as one of the best teams in the world. Scotland badly wanted to forget the difficulties they had endured in previous meetings and took up an invitation to return to Vienna and perhaps avenge their 5-0 defeat of 1931. They had just achieved a highly satisfying 3-1 win over England at Hampden Park and were confident. Yet again, though, the Austrians proved the better side and drew 1-1. Scotland's only excuse was that their right half, Alec Massie, was injured in the first ten minutes and had to move to the wing.

Hogan finished his work with the Austrian Olympic team and decided that he should again attempt to find employment back in England. Only one British club thought it was worth a gamble to employ a 54-year-old. They were told that it would be impossible for someone of his age to deal with young yet already established players, but the club had even taken the trouble to send a representative out to the Olympic Games in Berlin to open up negotiations. So in November, 1936 he took up Aston Villa's invitation to become manager. His decision had been made all the more difficult because one of his sons, Frank, was seriously ill with lung problems. Specialists said he would greatly benefit from living in a warm climate. By coincidence his father had been made offers to coach in Italy, but the approach by Villa and another, much more tentative and financially less interesting one by Arsenal, had more appeal. Villa offered him the greater control over the players.

At last he had another chance to prove that his coaching methods, which had brought him so much recognition and fame on the Continent, could be just as effective in Britain. But he was terribly torn between the health of his son and his yearning to prove that he could coach a home country team to success and finally be acknowledged where he most wanted recognition.

In the meantime the Austrians said that if he signed a new contract he could be employed for the rest of his career. The only proviso was that he would have to make his permanent home there. Circumstances prevailed. His son made a good recovery. The offer from Villa became irresistible.

After all of the travelling, he accepted that it was finished and he could look back on his time on the Continent with a sense of satisfaction heavily tinged with professional sadness. He said that while so much of it had been rewarding and enjoyable, the one thing he never got used to was the attitude of the European players towards defeat. He had seen grandstands being burned down, huge fights amongst spectators and even remembered an occasion in Hungary when the referee gave a penalty and a spectator came on to the pitch with a revolver and shot a bullet into the ball.

# OLYMPIC FARCE

Although deeply religious, he had been sickened by the ill-feeling between his Hungarian club MTK, which was predominantly Jewish, and FTC, which was mainly Christian. In one match between the clubs the police had gone on the field and arrested most of the MTK players. After an inquiry it transpired that the only reason for their action was that the inspector in charge was a FTC club member and his team were losing. Hogan was also horrified when the chairman of one of his clubs asked him to explain why at the end of a particularly good and competitive match he had congratulated the opponents who he said had won "fair and square".

# 14

# Villa Take the Risk

VILLA, WHO OFFERED HIM A three-year contract at £1,000 a year, were aware of the risk they were taking. His methods and dogmatic approach had resulted in fierce disagreements with several of the British players with whom he had worked in earlier years. He was unforgiving in his belief that the long ball game, played hopefully out of defence towards big, strong centre forwards, was not the route to success and, in any case, was less entertaining for the crowds than thoughtful football played through the middle of the field. Entertainment, he insisted, was the reason for the existence of professional football (something that many a modern manager still fails to acknowledge).

On his appointment he said: "At Villa Park I hope to accomplish even greater success. There is everything in my favour. I have experience: the Villa club has traditions second to none, and, above all, the material I have to work on possesses hereditary football ability. It will not be like manufacturing footballers, as I had to do in my earliest days of coaching on the Continent." But in spite of the fact that Villa's previous success had come about by employing the very tactical formation that Hogan always preferred, the directors were not at all convinced by his insistence that using the centre half as a third midfield player was the way forward at a time when most clubs had long since changed to having the stopper centre half. Neither did they believe that short passing and quick-slow movements played out of defence were likely to be rewarded. Chapman's thinking dominated the game. Hogan remarked: "Chapman was a great man but he had his ideas and I had mine."

Throughout his time coaching abroad he had one particular ally in Britain, the journalist John Macadam, who was probably the only person close to him who liked to believe that he was the embodiment of "modesty". Macadam never tired of mentioning his doubtful conclusion. He had been criticised by the football establishment for his effusive praise of Hogan's methods at the FA coaching courses but continued to support him and use his columns to emphasise his beliefs. Soon after the 1936 Olympics had ended he wrote in the Sunday Dispatch that Villa had "made the move of their life" in taking on Hogan after Arsenal had refused to give him a three-year agreement. But he anticipated problems. "There's bound to be a lot of the usual malicious and misinformed talk about English players knowing their own business best and about Continental methods. That's rubbish from the start. Jimmy Hogan is an English player using a super-intelligent development of English methods. That's all."

Hogan took over from Jimmy McMullan, who had been with Villa for only a year but left them in a comparatively depressed state. Straightaway he said all of the right things. He told Macadam: "I have read about the great Villa teams of the past. I have seen some of them, and I have even played against some of them. But this team we have got today is, in my opinion, the greatest team that Villa ever put on the field." It was a boast intended to raise confidence amongst the crowds as well as the players but was based on flimsy evidence.

For forty-eight years Villa had held a place in the top flight, but in the 1935-36 season they were relegated to the Second Division. Not only that, they conceded 110 goals. Their ability to turn their own ground into a fortress against visiting teams had disappeared. In one match, against Arsenal, Ted Drake had scored seven times. One of the Villa directors asked Hogan his opinion of the situation and, in particular, why so many clubs were playing a "big kicking game". Hogan replied: "I could not tell him why. I could only express my regret. The big kick must be scrapped. There's no question about it. A wild kick upfield is merely inviting the opposition to take possession of the ball." He said that possession football was nine-tenths of the game, adding: "It is the factor that overrides all others, and is the one which the Continentals have assimilated and put into practice." The Villa officials looked sceptical.

He gathered in new players, transferred a lot of others and changed the whole concept of how Villa's game should be played, once more stressing that the loss of possession was, in his eyes, a sin. The established players found it hard to accept that the hard, bruising game, with a lot of speculative balls played in the air, had no part in their new manager's tactical doctrine. The various changes led to a further period of uncertainty and by Easter it seemed that promotion was highly unlikely. The holiday programme brought them up against highly ambitious clubs: Newcastle away and at home and Blackburn away. But Hogan persuaded his struggling team that these matches offered the opportunity to show their real worth.

The talking worked. They beat Newcastle 2-0 at St James' Park and the following day Frank Broome achieved a hat-trick in the first half against Blackburn at Ewood Park. Blackburn stormed back in what Hogan described as "one of the most exciting games I ever saw". They recovered to 3-2 but finally lost 4-3. Meanwhile many of the teams in the top half of the division lost, so by Monday Villa were in a completely different situation. Incredibly, all they had to do was beat Newcastle on the Tuesday to become the division's leaders. Newcastle warmed to the challenge and won 2-0 at Villa Park.

# VILLA TAKE THE RISK

The spell had been broken and Villa drifted back down the table, finishing ninth.

In the early stages of his second season Villa took ten points from their first six matches and though they suffered a few setbacks, the team accepted him and his methods. The effect was to produce an entertaining side and a productive one - a combination Hogan always believed was what the public demanded. They were by far the best in the Second Division and won the title and promotion with a four point lead over Manchester United. Hogan also led them to the semi-final of the FA Cup in which they lost to Preston North End. Throughout, Eric Houghton, Frank Broome and Freddie Haycock formed the cornerstone of his team while Thomas Percival Griffiths was a centre half with such a natural ability to roam forwards in support of the attack that Hogan would regularly try to explain that, in the "modern" game, tactically there should always be a player who could both defend and attack from a central position. The 1970s showed how right he was with the emergence of Franz Beckenbauer who defined the role of the attacking sweeper.

The Villa board was still not won over. However, many of the players had cause to be grateful for Hogan's coaching. For instance, Houghton, who in spite of being a member of the England team, admitted that until the coach showed him he had little idea of how to carry out an effective body swerve.

In the middle of the 1937-38 season Hogan made his only appearance before the FA Disciplinary Committee following what the FA Minutes described as "incidents in the Leicester City-Aston Villa match on October 22". They fined him £5 and issued a reprimand for "unwarrantable conduct in the referee's room after the match". Three players were also cautioned. Hogan commented: "It is my first offence in football. Never before have I been before the FA either as a player, coach or manager. On those grounds I think I might have been dealt with less severely. I admitted that I went into the referee's dressing room after the match and expressed my opinion. However, my fine is paid and I am £5 the poorer. But the less said about it the better." He had been furious that one of his players was reported for leaving the field and returning without the referee's permission. His view was that the player had not stepped off the field of play. Trivial, perhaps, but in his opinion there had been an injustice reminiscent of the Olympic Games match against Peru.

He always maintained that the Villa side that won promotion out of the Second Division was as good as any he coached. They placed a great deal of emphasis on wingmanship, the quick counter-attack and accurate interplay. Besides going up, probably they should also have got to the Cup Final since they lost to a Preston goal that came after what Hogan claimed was "a glaring offside error on the part of the referee". The regular side was: Biddlestone; Callaghan, Cummings; Massie, Allen, Iverson; Broome, Haycock, Shell, Starling, Houghton.

At the end of the 1937-38 season Villa went on tour to Germany. Earlier the England team had controversially given the Nazi salute rather than appear to be rude to their hosts. The incident has often been alleged to have caused great resentment back in Britain, but in fact little was made of it in the Press since appeasement with Germany was the official Government line of the time. The Villa players were placed in a similar situation. Houghton and Broome had both been members of the England side that had been instructed by the FA to perform the salute but when he was asked whether he would do it for a second time, Houghton called a meeting of the team. Two of the Scottish players, George Cummins and Alec Massey, immediately said they would refuse. The rest of the team agreed not to salute.

Before a second match, in Stuttgart, Hogan again told the players that the club had asked them to give the Nazi salute.

# VILLA TAKE THE RISK

Houghton spoke to the group and pointed out that the Germans had made no protest about their earlier defiance, suggesting that it made no difference one way or the other. His team-mates reluctantly agreed that this time they would salute, except that they devised another way to show their objections. When the German arms went up, so did theirs, but to a man they put up two fingers which, according to Houghton, the cheering German fans totally failed to understand. At home the British public viewed the incident as a show of strength on behalf of the country's independence.

With war approaching, Villa finished twelfth in 1938-39. It was obvious that in future a full League programme would become impossible. In the following season the club completed only three games before war was declared. To help maintain the public's morale they, as with other major clubs, continued to play, often with teams augmented by servicemen who happened to be based in the area. Villa won the War Cup by beating Blackpool 5-4 on aggregate.

The club's chairman, Fred Normansell, was still unconvinced that it had been Hogan's methods that formed the basis of a revival or that they would serve them well after the war was over. Hogan himself had experienced scepticism so many times before. He heard Normansell say: "I've no time for all these theories about football. Get the ball in the bloody net, that's what I want." But there were happier days. On April 10, 1939 while still employed by Villa, he gave away his daughter Mary to Leo Riding, of Burnley, at St. Augustine's Church, Handsworth. His pleasure was mixed with worries that his future at Villa was in the balance, but his self-belief remained steadfast.

There was no point in attempting to argue with the anti-coaching officials, who doggedly refused to believe that England's declining record when playing against Continental opponents in their own countries had anything to do with an inability to accept that the game was changing and that the new generation had to be taught how to play the "foreigner" at his own vastly improved game. The facts against them should have been obvious:

May 15, 1929 (Madrid): Spain 4, England 3.
May 10, 1930 (Berlin): Germany 3, England 3.
May 14, 1930 (Vienna): Austria 0, England 0.
May 14, 1931 (Paris): France 5, England 2.
May 13, 1933 (Rome): Italy 1, England 1.
May 10, 1934 (Budapest): Hungary 2, England 1.
May 16, 1934 (Prague): Czechoslovakia 2, England 1.
May 6,   1936 (Vienna): Austria 2, England 1.
May 9,   1936:(Brussels): Belgium 3, England 2.
May 21, 1938 (Zurich): Switzerland 2, England 1.
May 18, 1939 (Belgrade): Yugoslavia 2, England 1.

A few months after the war began Villa said they could no longer retain him. Although he felt betrayed by the board members who doubted him, he could take some satisfaction from his record as manager: 126 games played, 57 won, 41 lost, 28 drawn, with 226 goals scored, 165 conceded and an average of 1.79 goals per game, which was a club record at the time. To their considerable credit the club agreed to pay him a pension that endured until his death.

# 15

# Back to Roots

HE DECIDED IT WAS TIME to return to where he had made his first steps on a long, often satisfying but ultimately frustrating football journey - to Burnley. Naturally, he offered his services to the club with whom he had always felt such a deep affection. They took him on and for the duration of the war used him in what he described as a "backroom capacity" which meant being little more than the elderly office boy but he soon gained the affection of local people. For instance, Barry Cragg, whose grandparents lived in the same street, recalled Hogan giving him "a real leather football which in those days was like gold dust".

Once the war was over and football had begun to get back to normal, with huge crowds revelling in the chance to be entertained after the years of deprivation, he more or less accepted that at his age he was not likely to be offered anything more substantial than the comparatively lowly position he already held at Burnley. He embarked on a lecture tour sponsored by the Daily Dispatch and was particularly warmly welcomed at St. Mary's R.C. Youth Club in Burnley. Amongst the audience of two hundred was the Burnley manager Cliff Britton together with several of the first team players. They knew all about his reputation as a coach but really only thought of him now as the "odd job man" around the club. They were amazed when he began to demonstrate how to control the ball.

# PROPHET OR TRAITOR?

It seemed as if he could talk it into doing his will, like a shepherd with his dog.

Then, out of the blue in September 1947, Brentford, who had been beaten in their first four Second Division games and were clearly struggling after the war had decimated their playing staff, made contact, asking him whether he was free to help them re-build. So, against all of his plans to settle back in Lancashire, he was again on the move. Upon his arrival back in the south he said: "I shall coach on modern lines similar to those I adopted with Villa before the war. Many of the methods used on the Continent are out of date now." He had accepted that the game was quicker, and while the need to have sound ball control remained essential, it had to be achieved at pace. After a month the News of the World reporter at a goalless home match against Cardiff City could still say: "The merit of Cardiff's performance was enhanced by the fact that they had the perhaps surprising experience of meeting with their most severe test so far, against a rejuvenated Brentford whose performance both delighted and encouraged their largest gate this season. To say Brentford's form was a revelation is hardly an apt description; it was just astonishing, and they have only to maintain it to be soon clear of the danger zone." Brentford finished the season in mid-table but by then Hogan had gone. He relished being seen to be capable of influencing an English league club in post-war football but suddenly came an even more unexpected opportunity - the chance to become full-time coach to Celtic where Jimmy McGrory was manager.

Among the young players recently signed was Tommy Docherty, who became and remained one of Hogan's most devoted followers. Docherty spent only one season with the club but believed it was the most important in the development of his career both as player and manager. He explained: "It was in the great days of Charlie Tully and players like that and they looked upon coaching as a bit of a joke. But Jimmy was a

152

fantastic man. I had come out of the Army in July, 1948 and reported to Celtic for pre-season training." In fact he need not have stayed in Scotland at all because Newcastle and Burnley had both made good offers to persuade him to go south of the border, but his ambition had always been to play for Celtic and no enticement would dissuade him.

He said: "A week later there were headlines saying they had signed this magnificent man who had coached the Austrian 'Wunderteam' and the Hungarians. All of them had been raving about him, but the Scottish players' attitude was: 'Who's this fellow then?'. I took to him very quickly, so did several of the other young players at Celtic Park at the time, but on the day of our first home game he sat us in the dressing room and said: 'This is the day the good ship Celtic will be launched'. One of the players said: 'You'll find a few passengers'."

Docherty was amazed at the confidence shown in him by Hogan, who saw him play in a tough reserve game against Rangers but asked him to appear in the first team the following day. Docherty had immediately made a good impression on the coach. He tackled well and was careful with his ball distribution. Like the other youngsters, he viewed Hogan as being almost ancient but he was enthralled by the "old man's" enthusiasm and practical ability. He explained: "He used to go around some of the other clubs a couple of nights a week talking and demonstrating, trapping and passing the ball. The great thing about him was his own personal performance in the coaching - his own technique. He would impress on everyone the need to be aware of what was going on around them before actually receiving the ball.

"He was a lovely man. He seemed dour but he had a lovely sense of humour. And he was a very religious Roman Catholic. He never swore or used any bad language at all. You could not possibly point a wrong word at him. That didn't go down well at Celtic Park with some of the players. These days we see players huddled together - bonding they call it - in the middle of the field before the game; well, Jimmy used to have them do that in the dressing room before we went out so it didn't cause any embarrassment out on the pitch. One or two of the older players looked at him as if to say 'what's this about?' but some of the younger ones like myself were all for it. We thought it was great.

"He always took a lot more time with the younger players because he saw them as the future of the club. I used to follow him two nights of the week to other clubs just to listen to him and watch him. I used to help him to demonstrate. I used to chip the balls up and he would trap and pass. His accuracy was magnificent. From thirty or forty yards he could hit a bucket - wonderful skill yet he was never what you would call a great player. But it's rubbish to say you've got to have been a great player to become a great coach and Jimmy was one of the people to prove that.

"He had a great influence over me. Before I joined Celtic I had been a centre half with junior sides. I'd played centre half all my life. He saw me as a wing half but first and foremost he saw me as a football player. He believed that all good players could play anywhere, barring the goalkeeper.

"As a person he was a gentleman of the highest order. But who gets on with all of the people all of the time? He set himself high standards and he expected everyone else to be the same. But he was never abrasive or lost his temper or anything like that. In fact if you wanted to criticise him you would have to say that he was too much of a gentleman. The fact that his work was never properly recognised in this country says a lot about our attitude to coaching and why we were so far behind the Austrians and Hungarians. These days you've got to have a coaching badge to get a job - well, Brian Clough, Jock Stein, Bill Shankly and Bob Paisley didn't and they didn't do too bad."

154

# BACK TO ROOTS

In his autobiography Docherty also recalled: "The best thing that happened to me at Celtic was the arrival of Jimmy Hogan to take over the side. This man was a wonder with youngsters. It's a bitter joke now, but the established stars would have nothing to do with him. Yet this was the man who went to the Continent and laid the foundations of the Hungarian's and Austrian's football. How blind can you be? But whatever the attitude of the 'big boys', I have never regretted that I took in every word Jimmy Hogan said. I reckon that I received my basic coaching from one of the greatest coaches the world has seen."

Docherty had a particularly personal reason to remember Hogan: "Apart from his help to me as a player, it was as a wise and understanding man that he perhaps kept me, a young man, on the straight and narrow path. I was among the selected Celtic squad that was sent to accept an invitation to the twenty-first birthday of a daughter of a friend of the club. Jimmy Hogan was in charge of us, and we were all under strict orders to report to him for the homeward journey at 10 p.m. I saw one girl, and fell for her. So much that I hardly left her all evening. Come 10 o'clock and I went to Jimmy to say 'Excuse me Mr. Hogan, but I have been dancing most of the evening with a certain young lady. She doesn't live very far from here, and so would you mind if I walked her home?' He looked at me from under his silver thatch, and said slowly: 'Well Tommy, suppose every player wanted to walk somebody home. If I said "yes" I'd be going back alone, wouldn't I?' 'Yes, Mr Hogan, but...' I started desperately. 'Well, you walk your young lady home this time, Tommy, but don't be late.' I scurried off to escort the future Mrs. Docherty home. It's a moot point as to what would have happened if Mr. Hogan had not given me his consent. I would have gone anyway, and the course of my future would have altered." Docherty went on to appear twenty-five times for Scotland and became one of the finest half-backs Britain has ever produced.

# PROPHET OR TRAITOR?

In many ways Hogan felt that taking on the job at Celtic was natural. Obviously, his Catholic and Irish background made him a suitable candidate. He said: "I feel at last that I have come hame (sic). I've mixed with Scots footballers ever since I kicked leather and such has been my admiration for their play that I have come to think of myself as a Scot." Even so, he told a local reporter from the Daily Record that he had sensed an air of suspicion amongst the players "as if each and every one was saying 'what can this old codger show us?'."

In another Daily Record article on August 5, 1948, the day after Hogan arrived, the columnist "Waverley" wrote: "Make no mistake about it, Jimmy is Scots by football adoption and has come here on a year's contract to help Celtic re-discover their traditional style of play. I watched him at work for two solid hours and marvelled that a man of his years - I reckon he has touched the sixty mark - should be so physically fit. He certainly carried out his maxim of not asking another fellow to do what he couldn't do."

The Scottish winger Johnny Paton was a member of the Celtic team Hogan coached. After his playing days ended he had a short period as manager of Watford but his most prized memories are of helping to develop several of the young Arsenal players who were to become the backbone of the League and FA Cup winning side of 1971. He and Docherty had been young players together at Celtic. He, too, recalled the memorable influence Hogan had over his career and a lifetime friendship. Yet he said that although Hogan was "a good man and he meant well and never did anyone a bad turn", he was "totally self-centred". He added: "Some people who knew him would say that he was full of himself; that's true. He was soaked in football and talked about nothing else, his family, friends or anything else. But as far as I was concerned that doesn't detract from his football knowledge. In later years he would come to our house in Stanmore and after a quick, polite reference to our family would sit down and talk about himself and his career for the rest of the afternoon. He never talked about his own family. We never met his wife. It was just football, football, football. Not that it wasn't interesting. He had a fascinating life but he had such a high opinion of himself that his autograph used to read 'Jimmy Hogan - the World's Number One Coach".

Like Docherty, Paton admitted that when Hogan arrived at Celtic he was looked upon as an unknown old man. "The attitude of the senior players was not very good, and that was disappointing. There was no doubt he was past his best but he was still a great demonstrator with a ball...he must have been wonderful when he was younger. His ideas were good and have never been bettered as far as I can say by anyone in the world. The reason he had been brought to Celtic was that we were a very young and inexperienced team. Celtic's policy was to rear their own players. They wouldn't buy them. As a result we were not getting good results and Rangers were winning everything. They bought players and had guests. Even Stanley Matthews played for them during the war.

"It was part of Jimmy's responsibilities to go round to the supporters' clubs and talk to them. It was not something I would have wanted to do, but I had the feeling that he wanted to do it for his own ego. I think he took a special interest in Tommy and myself and we used to go with him on his lecture trips. I think we were the two who were most interested in what he was doing. He used to say: 'The ball is round and it's meant to go round the team - play it simple and make it quick', which is exactly what Arthur Rowe was doing down at Tottenham. We Scottish players are always guilty of holding on to the ball too long. What stuck in my mind was his remark one day that the club didn't need a groundsman because 'we'll cut the grass with the ball'. The senior players laughed, but he was trying to get everyone into the mentality of keeping the ball on the floor, moving it quickly, making it simple and when not in possession get into position. England are still trying to do that and can't do what Jimmy was teaching us all those years ago. And I repeated what he told me all through my years of coaching.

"When I was coaching at Watford in 1953 I was still heavily influenced by Jimmy Hogan. I managed to get fourteen tickets behind the goal on the terraces for the Hungary game at Wembley and I told some of the younger players that I was taking them because it's going to be a football education. The boys hardly knew who Hungary were. I knew that the way Hungary had been playing was the way Jimmy had introduced way back in the Thirties. I still think that Hungary side was the finest I ever watched, and I've been involved in football all my life. And that team freely admitted that its greatest influence was Jimmy Hogan. He used to say 'Have you ever tried to open a tin of peas starting from the middle? How do you open a tin of peas from the middle of the can? You don't. You open it from the outside and that's the way you have to play. You have to make use of the width of the pitch and make progress down the outside and get down the line and cross because that's where most goals come from'. He knew that you had to be a great crosser of the ball. That's what makes David Beckham the player he is, and it's down to practice. Jimmy would have loved him."

While a convinced follower of Hogan's methods of coaching, Paton realised that the man had his faults, especially in his failure to maintain team discipline. "The older players had a very negative attitude and when he started asking them to hold hands in the dressing room before the game and concentrate on the job they were about to do, some of them would say: 'What's this old boy talking about?'. Now of course everyone does it from sports teams to people in industry. But at Celtic what he seemed incapable of realising or accepting was that the playing staff was not entirely Catholic. He talked as if they were and expected them all to go along with his religious beliefs. In that respect he was very naïve. You can't expect a whole group of footballers to go to Mass with you - but he did. But I don't want to say anything against him. He never did me a bad turn and he laid the foundations of football I still talk about today.

"He was too easy going and some of the players just couldn't see the point of what he was trying to do. He would often go and visit the players in their homes and talk football. He needed to be with football people all of the time. That's probably why he did so much talking to supporters' clubs. Without football he was a very lonely man. He was also so courteous that nobody ever had the heart to tell him to shut up. But he laid the foundations not only of the Continental game but our coaching in Britain because men like Walter Winterbottom and Ron Greenwood, both of whom managed England, followed his example. The West Ham "Academy" which Greenwood built around Bobby Moore and Martin Peters was based on the coaching initiative that Hogan had been teaching for years."

The highlights of Paton's time at Celtic mostly concerned Tully, whom he admired enormously. He recalled that in the almost unique atmosphere of the Celtic-Rangers "Old Firm" match Tully would put his foot on the ball and virtually invite two Rangers players to take it off him. Then he sidestepped them both. He gave Hogan credit for perfecting that technique.

Hogan's uneasy time at Celtic ended when Jackie Gibbons invited him back to join Brentford to help with the coaching work. He continued to warn that British football would soon be relegated by the Continentals. He would talk about it endlessly and then he turned to writing. In 1945 he had made a particularly impassioned plea for coaches to re-discover the skills that had once been automatic to the British players.

# PROPHET OR TRAITOR?

Writing in the Daily Dispatch on the eve of Moscow Dynamo's match against an Arsenal Invitation XI, he said: "We British are the best football players in the world. We are grand kickers of the ball, splendid headers, and possess the best sense of body balance. We are a race of natural football players. But what has happened of recent years to our game of football? Even before the war broke out few, if any, of our British touring teams were able to win a match in Austria, Hungary, Czechoslovakia or Italy.

"I have coached in almost every European country except Russia, but I know something about the Russians' football, too. Whilst coaching in Germany I saw Russian teams play there and was impressed by their speed and constructive carpet football. Still, before the war Russia was considered well down the list of Continental football. Surely she cannot have made such marvellous progress during the war years. The question is rather: are the Russians, Austrians etc. superhuman football players or has our own game deteriorated? My candid opinion is that our own game has gone back nearly 50 per cent. A bold statement to make, but I still maintain that we could beat any football team in the world if we would return to our old ideas of constructive play.

"We appear to have thrown our constructive and intelligent football aside and lapsed into a big-kicking, get-it-if-you-can game. Gone are the days when the ball went from man to man. What became of *our* carpet football? What about the old inter-changing of positions game? We taught the world how to do these things and then flung them away as if they were scrap. In these days of modern British football with four defenders, goalkeeper, full backs and centre half, we attack with practically a three-forward line, and the two inside men lying well in the rear.

"What has become of our beautiful wing game? The game which will spreadeagle any defence and draw the opposing

160

fullbacks out on to the touchline? In exchange for this we get the so-called down-the-middle style. In other words, booting the ball down the centre to the marked man and giving the opposing centre half every chance in the world to run on to the ball. This method is purely haphazard. It generally results in the fight for the ball in the air. Should the opposing centre-half make a mistake it may result in a goal-scoring chance for the centre-forward.

"Now, is this constructive or get-it-if-you-can football? You know the answer. I signed my contract for Aston Villa F.C. at the Olympic Games, Berlin, 1936. As soon as I had arrived in England I was told that the British game had been speeded up during my absence abroad, and that this generation demanded fast and thrilling football. This did not deter me in the least from carrying out my own ideas of constructive football played in a quicker manner. It can be done by intelligent players. I believe the Russians have given some fine demonstrations of this type of game. If we are to hold our own at our national game, we must scrap a deal of our modern ideas.

"I have seen League matches not worthy of the name football because there was not one iota of real football during the 90 minutes. Just aimless kicking of the ball and always hoping that the opposing defence would make a mistake. The average professional football player is not to blame. Very often he has to play to orders without being able to use his own initiative. But there are too many men leading the game who have not the foggiest notion of constructive and intelligent football. You know the type of man I mean; the one who walks into the dressing room and gives instructions such as 'Get stuck in lads, and swing the ball about'.

"There should be team meetings and discussions every week between the manager and his players to hold an inquest on the past games and to discuss plans for campaigns for the forthcoming one. Wake up England, and get back to the game."

# PROPHET OR TRAITOR?

Subsequently and significantly, Moscow Dynamo were unbeaten on their four match tour of Britain.

He summed up the whole of his career's attitude to coaching when writing in the magazine Sport Express: "Sometimes I have been accused of being a 'short passing' expert. This is ridiculous. Anybody who saw my Aston Villa side which won promotion and reached the semi-final of the Cup in 1938, must admit that we exploited the short pass, the long pass, the cross pass, the through pass, the reverse pass - in fact any other kind of pass which enabled us to keep possession of the ball...In the 'third-back game' and the exaggerated W formation, the very positions we take up on the field are forcing us into playing a high kicking game...Our very foundations have gone wrong. We must begin again with the boys at school. Impress it upon them that the ball should be played on the ground as much as possible, especially in approach work - and that football is a game of constructive and intelligent movements...I am not afraid to say that the records of men placed in such important positions as managers, trainers or coaches should be carefully examined and scrutinised before they are appointed.

"There is another important matter to be dealt with. Practically all over the Continent I have coached thousands and thousands of players with footballs, the object with which they must play all of their matches. We must have ball training, ball training and more ball training in this country until our players are complete masters of the ball...Of course, condition training is necessary, but the first thing for me is ball training! There are dozens and dozens of ball training exercises which will also get a player into condition...I maintain that every decent sized club should have a coach, but he must be an experienced, qualified one, who can put his football matter over and maintain discipline.

# BACK TO ROOTS

"We should also be careful not to rob a lad of his own natural ability to play the game. We should be patient and be more helpful than critical…Wake up England and play the game as it was intended to be played, intelligently, constructively. Then - and only then - we shall place ourselves back on top of the football world."

A lot of those sentiments remained true for fifty or more years afterwards. No doubt Hogan would have agreed that following England's worthy but misleading World Cup win of 1966, much of what he said became topical all over again, especially the greatly reduced emphasis on wingers and individualism. Harsh though it may seem to criticise Sir Alf Ramsey, his legacy had more to do with sheer, bloody-minded determination than ball-playing inspiration. England have too often come under the influences of misguided coaches who have based their philosophy on the mathematical chance that taking the most direct route to the opponent's goal leads to success. And just as bad, the majority of British born players in the Premiership at the beginning of the 21st century were still incapable of bringing the ball under control with real assurance or taking on more than one opponent.

# 16

# Seeing the Future

TO SUGGEST THAT HAD ALL of Hogan's theories been allowed to prevail, or that had he been permitted to coach at national level, everything in the English football garden would have been rosy is clearly to exaggerate. Also he was clearly wrong to suggest that in the early days few Continental players were poor finishers. View any old filmed record of their matches and there is proof that they frequently skied the ball high and wide. It took many years to improve them and Hogan's work encouraged rather than discouraged them to have a more patient attitude towards shooting than their British counterparts. What they sought was the ideal opening, which in football is a prized opportunity. The cat-and-mouse play of the 'Wunderteam' was an early example of the tactical initiative that later saw the European Cup dominated by Real Madrid and Liverpool.

Every now and again Hogan returned to the Continent to keep an eye on progress. In 1946 he went on a fifteen-day instructional course held by the French Football Association. He returned to report that it was the most thorough he had ever attended. Among the eighty coaches and players involved there were several from North Africa. The serious emergence of the African countries may still have been a few decades away, but he recognised the skill he saw amongst their players. Reiterating what he had said some years before when he spent a short time coaching in Tunisia, he remarked: "They are amongst the most naturally skillful footballers I have ever seen."

The course was led by the leading French coach Gabriel Hanot, who as football editor of the sports newspaper L'Equipe was later to be the guiding light for the founding of the European Cup. But Hogan was more impressed with Maurice Baquet who was an expert in "physical culture". Hogan called him "the most competent man I have ever seen." The routine on the course was punishing. Everyone had to be up by 5 a.m. Breakfast consisted of a black coffee and bread. The day's instruction began at 6 a.m. with talks about the theory of football, followed by exercises. In the afternoon there were written examinations and discussions about the practical work that had been done in the morning. Hanot acted as examiner. Only twenty passed and received the French FA diplomas which entitled them to coach at any of the clubs in the French league. Twenty- six received second class certificates and were invited to return the following year. In the meantime their coaching work was to be restricted to amateur teams. Hogan said that his own contribution to the course was "giving humble demonstrations".

In spite of many articles in national newspapers suggesting that his talent was being wasted, to make ends meet he had to do mundane things, such as holding part-time coaching courses at Southend Football Club. Among the journalists of the day who felt strongly that he was being neglected and said he had been impressed by the intensity of the French coaching ideas was Ernest Edwards, who commented that it was no wonder that England had been beaten in Switzerland and France and only drawn against "little Belgium". He said that English football had never seen anything like the French course. Echoing Hogan's familiar cry, he said: "Wake up, England. Get back to intelligent and constructive football."

# PROPHET OR TRAITOR?

Unhappily, Edwards' advice was not heeded and English football's insularity was made doubly unforgivable by the fact that another enormously gifted manager-coach, George Raynor, was also lost to the country. Raynor had a remarkable career abroad. He guided Sweden to an Olympic gold medal in 1948, ironically in England at Wembley, and to bronze in 1952. While England were being embarrassed by their defeat against the United States in the 1950 World Cup, he was coaching Sweden to third place. Eight years later in Stockholm he took them to the final in which, understandably, they lost to the Brazilian super-talents of Pele, Garrincha, Vava and Didi. The Brazilians were so impressed that they gave him a gold medal. The King of Sweden made him Knight of the Order of Vasa, and Raynor stayed to mastermind a 3-2 away win over England in 1959. It was only England's third defeat on home soil.

Back in England Raynor was hardly recognised. He shared that situation and much else with Hogan. He came from a poor background. He was born in 1907 and within a short time his father, a miner, was out of work. Although his first jobs were as a butcher's apprentice and lorry driver, he was a talented footballer and was a professional for seventeen years. During the First World War he was an instructor in the Physical Training Corps after which he concentrated on football coaching, first with Iraq's national side. Even so, he, like Hogan, would have been happy to coach one of the major English clubs but no offer came. Obscurely, rather than encouraging him to stay in Britain, Stanley Rous recommended him to the Swedish FA.

Given too little time with the Swedish national team's players, Raynor decided to visit their clubs and assist with their coaching, much in the way Hogan had travelled to the players rather than always expecting them to come to him. Finally he left Sweden for Italy where he coached Juventus and Lazio, but he was unhappy about corruption. His final job as a manager was at Doncaster Rovers, who he took into the Second Division, but by then he was in his sixties and finally he was reduced to being a storeman at Butlins holiday camp at Skegness. His career was such that he could claim to be the most successful English international manager, but he would never do so. His modesty and humility perhaps worked against him. On the other hand Hogan could hardly be accused of modesty yet he, too, was looked upon with suspicion by most of the leading English officials.

The experience of being shunned by their own country was one that Raynor and Hogan shared with many others. British coaches who went abroad were soon forgotten at home. Jesse Carver, Ted Crawford and Leslie Lievesley all worked in Italy, John Dick and John Madden were employed in Prague, and as early as 1912 Bill Garbutt was coaching Genoa to the Italian championship. His story is worth a book in itself. He joined up with the British Army in 1918 but afterwards returned to Italy to take charge of Napoli and Roma. He moved on to Spain and led Bilbao to the title before the Civil War began. He was extradited, with virtually no money, but made his way back to Italy where he trained AC Milan. He lost his wife and family in an allied bombing raid yet decided to join the Italian resistance. Once the war was over he returned to Genoa and resumed coaching.

Hogan spent a few months going back to his family roots, travelling around the north and south of Ireland discovering young players. He predicted that Ireland would produce some of the most skillful players of the future, and was proved right, not least, of course, in George Best. At the time the Eire FA offered him a job as the national team's coach but after long deliberation and considering his advanced years, he decided that an opportunity to move to Brentford was more appropriate, but it was a tough decision for a man proud of his Irish ancestry.

# PROPHET OR TRAITOR?

He felt obliged to coach youth players because they were the future of the game. However, he said: "I thought long and hard before I decided, regretfully, to turn down this offer, but at Brentford one of my old boys, Jackie Gibbons, is manager and he and I have similar ideas. Jackie has gradually brought along a string of youngsters and I am convinced that we have the material to make a first class team. I have always maintained the answer to soccer success is to find your own youngsters when they are still in their teens and bring them along. That is also Jackie Gibbons' idea and between us I am sure we can build a team to take Brentford back to the First Division, and in double quick time. I am approaching the end of my career now, and I can think of no better way to complete my soccer saga."

He certainly put strenuous efforts into the task but, again, others failed to agree with his methods and he left the club. He became frustrated and worn down mentally. His enthusiasm for football itself remained sparkling fresh but he felt unwanted by its people. He told Alan Hoby, of The People: "I feel that I have been pushed aside. I have been turned down by Manchester City and Sheffield Wednesday." Hoby commented: "Why has he been pushed aside? Maybe because in this speed-drunk age, with a new high in transfer hysteria sweeping the game, Hogan is against the four-figure buy, he believes in building from the bottom."

An application to coach Blackburn Rovers failed. Hoby's response was: "His record? So brilliant you need sun-glasses to view it. This column therefore asks: can English football - now practically on its knees to the Continentals - afford to ignore for the sake of quick results, big transfers and easy money, such a first-rate brain?" The plea brought no response from any of the British clubs.

Hogan then did the unthinkable and dropped out of top class football altogether. He was invited by the Dispatch to

168

visit schools and youth clubs in Lancashire to give talks and demonstrations. He travelled some six thousand miles and taught thousands of youngsters. However, he later confessed: "What a shock I had. I discovered that at least half of my pupils did not know that the ball should be kept 'on the carpet' as much as possible. They were under the impression that the 'leather' should be kicked in the air and chances taken. With regard to constructive and intelligent movement, they were very backward. So don't ask me why the Continentals are beating us at our own game. It is perfectly obvious that our own football foundations are crumbling."

In his cogent book Soccer Nemesis, which examines British football's failure to react to the challenge from the Continent, the journalist Brian Glanville told of a personal experience. "One seemed to be watching the very essence of Hogan's career at a coaching demonstration which he gave in 1952. It took place in the bleak, sad hall of a council school in West London, pregnant with cold, bare corridors, knowledge grudgingly imparted and still more grudgingly received, stone playground, compulsory milk, and young teachers who would eventually turn it all into a best-selling novel. There was a sparse evening audience of small boys and disgruntled adults; a cantankerous little Welshman complaining about the BBC. Amidst this meagre audience, beneath the pale and insufficient light, Hogan appeared, a rebuke to them all; close on seventy, silver-haired, dressed in a bright green Celtic track suit, wonderfully alert and eager, an Olympian among pygmies.

"He demonstrated how to kick a ball, and hit the same spot on the wall one, two, three…seven times in impeccable succession, until even the small boys and the gloomy men applauded. He called them all, affectionately, 'my dear friends', he occasionally told stories against himself. "I was giving a lecture to troops in France, in 1940, and kept telling them to keep the ball 'on the carpet'. When I'd finished and asked for questions, a voice said from the back, 'What happens if you come to a ground where they haven't got a carpet?'." He reaffirmed several times his belief that British footballers were potentially the best in the world, then put a handful of young professionals through their paces, and finished the evening looking as fresh and active as the youngest of them."

On the Continent the name of Hogan was not forgotten. Gusztav Sebes invited him to return to Hungary and help with some coaching at the army club Honved, which had been formed by the Hungarian Ministry of Sport in 1949 and was based in Budapest. Sebes had taken the existing players of the Kispest club which was housed in a suburb of Budapest. Then he scoured the country looking for more talent. For the next seven years Honved dominated Hungarian football, winning five championship titles and being runners-up twice. The leading goalscorers were Ferenc Puskas and Sandor Kocsis who, together with the fine goalkeeper Gyula Grosics, were to become the central figures in the outstanding Hungarian national side and names never to be forgotten in England. They were constantly reminded of Hogan's theories: simple passing and the constant search for open space; theories that he had preached unrelentingly and which had found little sympathy among British teams he coached.

Sebes and Hogan had much in common, not least their poor early lives. In his youth Sebes went to France as a guest-worker which brought him a meagre wage. His outlet was football, playing for a colliery team in Bordeaux. As with Hogan he was skillful but not totally successful as a player. He won one cap for Hungary before becoming their coach.

# 17

# Back to Villa

CURIOUSLY, IT WAS IN OCTOBER of that most significant year of 1953 that Eric Houghton, who had only recently been appointed manager of Aston Villa, suggested to Hogan that he joined him. He wanted to improve the standards of the youth team and felt that his old friend, even at 71, not only had the experience but retained the ability to teach and animate his young players. At the time Ron Atkinson, later to become manager of Manchester United and, more recently, the respected and witty senior member of ITV's team of football experts, was a junior player with Villa. Hogan impressed him enormously.

He recalled: "He came to look after the 'A' or third team in the Birmingham League. I would say that his coaching was revolutionary at the time. Everything we did we did with a ball, which was foreign to coaching in those days. We used to practice on a tarmac car park, taking the ball with the inside of your foot, the outside, your other foot, pass and run…all things I've seen people do in latter years, but prior to that I don't think it had ever been done in this country. When we had a practice game everyone loved playing in his team because his basic theory was that whenever we had the ball, wherever we were on the field, we were all attacking. When they had the ball we were all defending. That was his stock in trade.

# PROPHET OR TRAITOR?

"Everyone had responsibility when we lost the ball but when one of our team had it he would say that we had to give him lots of options. So it was never one-dimensional. It was a form of Total Football if you like. He would say to the wing halves 'You are the waiters - you have to provide the service for the people who want to eat'. He had lots of little sayings like that, and even now when you see teams like Liverpool going into a huddle before a game, I remember he used to have us doing that.

"One of the things he used to show us was how to take the ball one way, put your foot over it and drag it back on the other side and come back out the other way. It's difficult to explain and I didn't see many players do it but in more recent years one who did was Frans Thijssen and when he did it I always used to think 'yes, that was the one Jimmy used to show us'. Jimmy used to say that you had to treat the ball kind. He used to have us putting our foot on it and gently roll it back. But then when we moved up from the 'A' team to the reserves there would be this old cloth cap trainer and he would say 'forget what bloody tip-taps told you, give it some altitude'. But everyone else had the utmost respect for Uncle Jimmy.

"You talk about people being ahead of their time, well he was certainly that but whether people would have been receptive to him in this country in earlier years is difficult to say. But it was only after the Hungary match in 1953 that people were shaken and began to say 'now hold on a bit'. In the years before that possibly they may not have received his ideas so easily.

"I shall always remember how, even when he was in his seventies, he could demonstrate what he wanted you to do. A load of the things he did I always kept in my locker. He was such a marvellous person. People called him Uncle Jimmy and he was like an uncle. You always looked forward to being in his group. I can't remember him ever once raising his voice, but he got all of the respect."

172

# BACK TO VILLA

Among the other young players Hogan taught was Peter McParland, the Irish winger, who was to score ninety-eight league goals in two hundred and ninety three appearances for Villa between 1952 and 1961 and was a member of the fine Northern Ireland side that reached the quarter-finals of the World Cup in 1958.

McParland remembered that at the time he wondered how "this quiet man who never raised his voice and never swore" had become such an influence in Europe. But he was totally beguiled. "He was such a dainty sort of man, a lovely man, decent, almost pious in his ways. He brought something new to me - I was allowed to train more with the ball. To my mind he was way ahead of his time. The sort of ball work that is done now amongst the best teams, Jimmy Hogan was doing that years before. He even used a little ball to improve control, which you sometimes see being used today.

"When I came over from Ireland, in training all the trainer would say was 'kick it'. Danny Blanchflower was at Villa at the time and he used to cry out 'We want the ball'. But there was still the idea that if you trained too much with the ball during the week you wouldn't want it on Saturday. But Jimmy didn't think like that and it was like fresh air to us lads. I'm a Catholic and he would come into the dressing room and put the rosary beads close to me - he was almost holy in his ways."

Before arriving at Villa McParland had thought of himself as an inside forward, but it had been a condition of his transfer from Dundalk that he played at outside left. He said: "I just could not get the hang of that outside left position. My big failing was that I kept waiting for the ball instead of going back for it. I was struggling and I began to feel I'd missed my chance. It was the vital point in my career. I know of many youngsters who have reached the same stage and have lost confidence and drifted out of the game. Again, I was lucky. Villa's famous coach took me under his wing. Whenever my confidence showed signs of flagging, he was there to boost me up again with a few words of advice.

"Jimmy was a great character. He carried on coaching at Villa Park until he was seventy-six, and even at that age he could do anything with a ball except make it talk. It was a real inspiration to the youngsters to watch him. It was Jimmy's idea to switch me to left half to help me on a bit, and for quite a spell I stayed at wing half, playing in every game possible in the reserves, third team and Midland Mid-Week League side."

Unlike McParland, Ken O. Roberts, who was also a talented junior player with him at Villa, had only a short career in the first team because it was cruelly ended by a cruciate ligament injury of the sort that over the years has destroyed the hopes of so many players. In spite of still being in plaster and fearing that his career was at an end, he was persuaded by Hogan to join the other young players on the coach to Wembley. He was stimulated by what he saw but when, eventually, he was able to play again, he was involved in only two more games before it was obvious to him and the club that his future was not as a player.

Roberts had only a short time in which to come under Hogan's spell, but the experience stayed with him for so long that he would use it when, between 1968 and 1976, he became the successful manager of Chester City and in recent years as coach of Shrewsbury Town's young players. "He seemed like a father-figure to me, but when I look back I realise what an influence he could have been on the English game. My first reaction was - he's an old man, though, I suppose not much older than I seem to the young players I coach now. Then I realised he was different. He had a gift for putting things over so that it was once told never forgotten.

"The things he told me then I can reflect on now and tell the youngsters. I know people may say that what he told me was a long time ago and the game is different now, but at the end of the day it was then, and is now, all about playing with a ball. That may sound obvious but even in the 1950s the ball was not often used in training.

"I think at first the senior players kept Jimmy at a distance, but the nature of the man soon won everyone's respect. When they found out about his achievements they began to realise what he had done. I think you had to sit down and talk with him to appreciate the gift that he had and what he could give us. He made us all better players.

"In those days we had a trainer who would say 'right, this is what we'll do today', and that meant no work with the ball after Wednesday. He still believed in the old idea that if we trained without it for a few days we would be more hungry for it on Saturday. And that wasn't happening just with us at Villa but everywhere else. But when Jimmy came there were footballs everywhere and, of course, no one can resist a football. That had a big effect on the way training went for us, but we were lucky.

"As a person Jimmy was very reserved when he was with us, very private but quite outgoing when he was training. He gave you confidence. He was an absolute gentleman. I can't remember anyone who didn't in the end respect him. There was hardly ever any bad language, otherwise you got a clip round the ear. He didn't make it obvious that he was a religious man but it was something we sensed. When I say we didn't swear when he was about, I mean that it was not because he told us not to but because when he was about we felt it would be wrong. It was always like being with your dad. We would have understood why abroad he was known as 'Uncle Jimmy'.

"He was an exceptional person but he never said anything to us about what he had done in the past. It was all something we found out from other people as we worked with him, so we came to respect him for it. We began to realise how important he had been.

# PROPHET OR TRAITOR?

"I got into the first team when I was only seventeen. I remember there was one day when we were in the dressing room and it must have been obvious to him that I was getting nervous. He pulled me to one side and said he was going to say something that he hoped would stand me in good stead. It turned out to be the most sound advice I ever had as a player and afterwards. He said: 'Over the course of your life, not only in football, you will have a lot of people coming to you with advice. Always be willing to accept it and be a good listener. Let the good stick with you and let the bad go right through.' That's something that to this day I talk to the boys about. I was very young when he said that to me but I never forgot it because he was a man who had a presence.

"We never did anything untoward when he was around. In fact, for footballers, we were probably a bit prim and proper. That was because of the respect we had for him. We reacted to the fact that we never saw him in a temper or seeming to be frustrated when we didn't achieve what he wanted. I'm sure that at other clubs that may have worked against him, especially with the senior players and coaches. But I think Jimmy realised that Peter McParland and I had, what they say in football is 'good feet'. We could strike the ball well and we were both inside forwards originally but became wingers. Jimmy must have had an influence on that decision which was made by the manager, Eric Houghton. Jimmy really believed in wingers.

"He was a believer in pure football. If he had been given the opportunity he would have made a major contribution to the game in this country. In spite of his age, he could have been a big influence after the 1953 match when we all realised that we had to do something positive about our football. A lot of people at the time ought to have tapped into what he had being doing. Even now we still fail to trust players with skill. We still haven't grasped their value."

# BACK TO VILLA

The warnings ought to have been plain to see, especially after England had suffered the shocking defeat by the United States in the World Cup of 1950. The excuses for England's decline in world standards were limitless but Sir Stanley Rous was not inclined to believe any of them. He had gone to Helsinki in 1952 and watched the Hungarians win the Olympic gold medal with a style of possession football that had first been seen in the days when Hogan was their inspiration. It was Sir Stanley's idea to invite them to England at about the time of the Football Association's 90th anniversary, but ahead of that England played a FIFA XI (October, 1953) which, although lacking South American players, nevertheless exposed the faults. A 4-4 draw was achieved only because Alf Ramsey scored late in the game from the penalty spot.

Among the players who had magnificently decorated the match was the attacking centre-half Ernst Ocwirk, an Austrian who had been taught in the Hogan tradition of the "Viennese School" of football. He had first been seen in England during the Olympic Games of 1948 and played a crucial part when Austria returned to Wembley in 1951 and drew 2-2 - one of so many warnings that went unheeded. Another superb performance was also seen from Ladislao Kubala who scored twice for the FIFA XI, though both from the penalty spot. He, too, was a product of Hungarian football based on Hogan's teaching. And, incidentally, he played for three different countries: Hungary, where he was born, Czechoslovakia, where he represented Bratislava, and Spain, the country to which he was later naturalised.

What impressed more than anything about England's match against the FIFA side was how well the visiting group of players, drawn from several different countries, gelled. There was no secret, certainly not to Hogan who watched the game. He pointed out that each player had supreme ball control. In the words of Geoffrey Green "they had mastered the basic

# PROPHET OR TRAITOR?

grammar of the game; they were able to speak its language at a higher level". He added that England "snatched our goals by enthusiastic harrying; they by scientific, creative planning".

A few players in the English league regularly joined Hogan in warning about what would happen if coaching to the Continental standards was not quickly adopted. Tommy Lawton, the formidable England centre forward of the 1930s and '40s, was one. He wrote: "When I toured Switzerland in 1946 and saw the mass coaching that was taking place there, I said that within five years we in Britain would be playing second fiddle to the Continentals unless something was done quickly. People laughed at me then, but I was only two years wrong. Our slide became more and more apparent as the years went by, but it was not until 1953 that we took what was the real knock-out punch…the 6-3 defeat at Wembley by Hungary."

"Many people were horrified at this result and went hysterical. Yet those very same people had done nothing about the Continental challenge that had been building up. In fact they had denied its existence. Other people took another, but equally dangerous view. They stupidly insisted that we could still lick the hide off the Continentals, and, as if to contradict themselves, trotted out all sorts of phoney excuses for our defeats. The most popular one was 'the war', but that had long outlived its usefulness as an excuse for our failures, if, indeed, it had ever been a valid excuse."

Lawton entirely agreed with Hogan about football in England having its head in the sand. He wrote: "We forgot that the Continentals were all the time perfecting the art of the game, advancing the tactics and the moves. They were, in fact, slowly but surely mastering the craft of soccer. And what were we doing all this time? Going along our own sweet way to self-destruction. We didn't think anyone had anything to teach us. We didn't want to learn. Our tactics became out of date. We got into a rut."

# BACK TO VILLA

As with many other senior players of the early post-war years, Lawton went abroad to coach and played an important part in the emergence of Holland as a power in world football. He coached Sparta, of Rotterdam, whose players had only just turned from amateur to semi-professional. Like Hogan in an earlier era, he was amazed by the enthusiasm of the foreign players but felt hurt and embarrassed at having to leave his own country to teach on the Continent. He wrote: "But why should I and other players have to go abroad to get coaching appointments? Isn't there sufficient work for us to do here at home? I am convinced there is. The tragedy of the game is that we have allowed so many of our fine players to go out of the game instead of using them as coaches. That would never be allowed on the Continent where they utilize every scrap of brain in their fight to become proficient and super proficient."

Hogan became ever more frustrated that the English league was fixed in what he called "Victorian ideas", which continued to have too little regard for those players who had real ability and left the professionals with too much time on their hands. In the early 1950s, this was a typical week in the life of a professional in the first division, and, apart from a visit to a cinema, clearly it had changed very little from the schedule followed by clubs in the early part of the century:

Monday: Day off. Usually spent at home. Alternatively, a visit to the cinema, golf course or the pub.

Tuesday: Report to the club at 9.30 a.m. A couple of laps running round the pitch followed by a six-a-side. Some players worked together on what would now be called "set-pieces". Ten minutes in the gym jumping over a vaulting horse. Lunch in the club canteen (Menu: Sausage-toad and two veg, syrup pudding). Manager's talk. Afternoon free.

Wednesday: If wet, play a six-a-side game under one of the grandstands. If dry, on the pitch. Members of the winning side rewarded with twenty cigarettes. Treatment for injuries. A few laps round the edge of the pitch. Afternoon free (some players helped coach at local schools).

Thursday: Cross-country run lasting about half an hour. Occasional visit to a seaside resort to run on the beach and have lunch at a local hotel (one player of the time said there was usually a five-course lunch finishing with waffles and ice cream: "Except for before a match, a footballer should eat just what he fancies.").

Friday: "Spike work" in the morning (running in athletics shoes) followed by a six-a-side game or if the following day's match was away, board the coach or train for the journey. Early night, probably after a visit to the cinema.

Saturday: Spend the morning playing cards. Light lunch (usually fish). Arrive at the ground an hour before kick-off. Players with slight injuries have massage. Some, but not all, spend a few minutes "limbering up" in the dressing room. The manager offers a few words of advice about the opposition. After the match, no warming down, just a quick exit for the station.

Sunday: Visit the ground for treatment, if necessary. Otherwise down to the pub for Sunday lunch.

Such a complacent attitude to preparation defied all of the evidence of an impending shift in the balance of power. Britain was about to fall behind Europe and Europe was to bow to South America. After the Second World War the mood of the country was for change, except, it seemed, amongst the influential people in football who simply went about their business as if the warnings of Hogan, Meisl and their teams could be dismissed as part of a past era. The early international matches of the post-war years suggested that they had a point. England had resumed with a 7-2 away win over Northern Ireland in which Billy Wright made his debut. Then there were comfortable wins over Belgium, the Netherlands, France and Portugal. But there was one glitch: defeat, albeit by a single goal, to Switzerland in Zurich. That was easily forgotten with a 4-0 victory over Italy in Turin in 1948. Everything seemed to be providing solid evidence that Hogan's foreboding was nothing more than bitter resentment at his personal treatment by English football.

Although the FA did agree to rejoin FIFA, their attitude towards the 1950 World Cup was that England would hardly need any special preparation to prove that they were the best team anywhere. Hogan said at the time that he was convinced that even if they did well against other European sides, the South Americans "may have something to show us". He had been supported in his reservations by England's 1949 defeat by Sweden in Stockholm and the 2-0 home defeat by the Republic of Ireland at Goodison Park.

The finals were an administrative fiasco, with several countries pulling out, including Scotland, after they were faced with absurd distances to travel between matches. Curiously, the Austrians, in spite of being brought up on the theories put forward by Hogan, decided not to go because they felt their team was not sufficiently experienced. Not only that, the competition was deeply weakened and saddened by the absence of Italy. Their team had been decimated by an air crash. Seventeen Torino players died - the nucleus of the national side. In addition, the wise Vittorio Pozzo had been dismissed as technical director.

In spite of the fact that their gifted centre-half Neil Franklin had accepted an offer to play in Colombian football and decided against appearing in the World Cup, England still had what should have been a formidable side, including Stanley Matthews (who, amazingly, was only added at the last minute), Stan Mortensen, Tom Finney, Wilf Mannion, Billy Wright and Alf Ramsey. It was no surprise that England were seen as joint favourites with Brazil. Hogan remarked: "I have not had the good fortune to go to South America, but I know what these players can do. They play correctly…on the ground." He was impressed to hear that the Brazilian squad was accompanied by three chefs and a doctor. He was also aware that the Swedish team had their English coach, George Raynor, in charge, and admitted to a little jealousy.

Hogan's suspicion that the Brazilians, who had looked full of skill but lacked organisation back in 1938, were now a force to be feared was proved correct. They comfortably beat Mexico 4-0 in the gigantic, new Maracana Stadium. Meanwhile Raynor inspired his Swedish side to a 3-2 win over Italy before they drew with Paraguay, which allowed them to go through to the next phase. England had beaten Chile 2-0 in their opening game but they had struggled physically in the heat of Rio.

Then England faced a match that in many ways was almost as significant as the 1953 defeat by Hungary. Even Hogan failed to foresee any danger in a confrontation with the United States, who were captained by Eddie McIlvenny who had been given a free transfer from Wrexham, then of the Third Division North, in the year before. The American team was a hotchpot. They had a defender from Belgium, a centre forward from Haiti and several players who had virtually no experience of playing in Europe or against top class opposition. Yet in Belo Horizonte the biggest surprise in the history of the game thus far came about. The coach of the US team, Bill Jeffrey, originally from Scotland but working at Pennsylvania University, told journalists from Britain that he had little hope of his team doing anything more than not disgracing themselves. As for his players, they were so convinced that they were about to be trounced that they spent most of the night before the game drinking and playing cards.

Amazingly the United States won. Admittedly the pitch was in poor condition and facilities less than acceptable, but

# BACK TO VILLA

England's defeat was of their own making. First there was the complacency, then terrible failings in front of their opponent's goal. The American goalkeeper, Borghi, was invincible and the defence backed him up with surprising composure. The US scored in the 37th minute when Behr sent the ball across the penalty area and Larry Gaetjens, the Haitian, headed past Bert Williams. Jimmy Mullen later seemed to head the ball across the goal-line from Alf Ramsey's free kick but the States held on to their single goal for victory.

England were left needing to beat Spain in Rio to remain in the competition. They made several changes. Matthews was brought back and Eddie Baily and Bill Eckersley made their first appearances. However, Spain won 1-0 and England went home while Brazil overwhelmed Raynor's Sweden by seven goals, although the Swedes went on to take third place as a result of a 3-1 win over Spain. Brazil lost in the final to Uruguay but did enough to point a finger at the direction in which world football was to take.

Back at home, England's degradation at the hands of the United States was not taken seriously. Media coverage of the competition had not been comprehensive and the conclusion was that the result was one of those strange ones that happen in football. In reality, England had been found wanting in their first attempt at competing in world-wide competition. The warnings that Hogan, and others, had been repeating were still ignored. But the evidence continued to grow. Argentina visited Wembley in 1951 and held a 1-0 lead until the seventy-ninth minute. England grabbed two goals and satisfaction ruled. Austria came and drew 2-2. England also met a Rest of Europe team in October, 1953 and were saved only by a last minute penalty by Ramsey which balanced the score at 4-4. A month later came the Hungarians.

# 18

# "England to Slam Hungary"

WHEN HOGAN ASKED VILLA whether he could take his young players to Wembley to see Hungary's match against England he told the club, and them, that he could promise they would witness something to open their eyes. Indeed they did. And the eyes of the nation suddenly saw the light.

In anticipation of the game there had been some chauvinistic talk by those who should have known better. Among them was Charlie Buchan, the former England, Sunderland and Arsenal player who in his day was an inventive inside forward but had conspired with Herbert Chapman to create the "stopper" centre half. Hogan and Buchan never saw eye to eye. Buchan wrote in the New Chronicle: "I think we have the men to beat the brilliant Hungarians. This is the best team England have put in the field this season." He said the close ball control and accurate passing of the Hungarians did not worry him at all. "Close marking by the half backs is the answer", he claimed, adding that the defenders should prove equal to the task.

One always shrewd critic and no bad amateur player in his day thought otherwise. The perceptive Geoffrey Green told listeners to a radio programme: "One of these days we shall wake up and find six goals in the back of the net. I believe Hungary will beat us 4-2." Even he underestimated the depth of the gulf that had been sunk between England and the best national team from the Continent.

184

# "ENGLAND TO SLAM HUNGARY"

Hogan was convinced that everything that had happened in the run-up to the historic match pointed to the fact that Hungary would thrive on their years spent concentrating on ball skills, the effective use of space and the counter-attacking game. Clearly in England the priorities had hardly moved on from pre-War days. Yet the national team went into the 1953 match content that they had nothing to fear. By and large the national press felt sure England would win. Geoffrey Green knew his football history and was familiar with Hogan's achievements with MTK. He was in a small minority to caution against believing in a foregone conclusion. His preview in The Times included the thought that England should expect to be "taken to the last ditch and possibly beyond".

On the morning of the match the Daily Telegraph took a slightly more optimistic line by suggesting that Matthews and the inexperienced George Robb could be match winners. The other papers also predicted an England victory. The Daily Mail went as far as to have a headline saying: "England players to slam Hungary - and critics". The Daily Herald confidently went in favour of England, as did the Daily Express. The Daily Sketch suggested that their readers put "a bob" on England, which in those days was not an insignificant wager. Most surprising of all, though, was the fact that the Daily Worker made no attempt to be loyal to their Communist brothers from the east and carried the headline "England to win". Other headlines that day included: "Hard Tackling The Way To Beat Hungary" and "Hungary's Fancy Stuff Won't Beat England".

Even the usually astute George Raynor sent a message to one of the Sunday newspapers saying: "After seeing the Hungarians last Sunday, I am convinced that playing in the old British style and spirit England's footballers can win at Wembley on Wednesday." However, he added the warning: "England's opponents are weak in defence but have a strong, clever forward line. Their key man is centre-forward

# PROPHET OR TRAITOR?

Hidegkuti…The Hungarian forwards are extremely good at passing and inter-passing and fast at re-positioning…England must win to maintain the prestige abroad of fellows like myself." Only a minority of journalists had the foresight to emphasise that they thought it might be a close game.

The defeat was the result of failure to move with the times and absurd over-confidence amongst the players (famously the captain, Billy Wright, turned to Stan Mortensen as they walked out side by side with the visitors and said: "We should be all right here, Stan, they haven't even got the proper kit."). In later life he admitted: "In hindsight, that was the daftest thing I ever said." In those days none of the English players wore the low cut, lightweight boots preferred on the Continent, let alone the short shorts.

England's selection was curious but still, in theory, formidable. Tom Finney had withdrawn injured and Robb, a former amateur international who was in only his first season as a professional with Tottenham Hotspur, replaced him for his first cap. In all probability he was chosen more for what he knew than what he could do. Robb had been in the British Olympic team, so had at least seen some of the opposition. There was some criticism of the choice of forwards since Nat Lofthouse had been omitted to make way for Mortensen (probably because of his Blackpool partnership with Matthews which had been so successful in the "Matthews Final" earlier in the year) and Ernie Taylor, also of Blackpool, took over from the mercurial Albert Quixall for his first and only international appearance. In the event, however, it was not the attack that was found wanting but the defence and half backs.

The England team was: Merrick (Birmingham City); Ramsey (Tottenham Hotspur), Eckersley (Blackburn Rovers), Wright (Wolverhampton Wanderers), Johnstone (Blackpool), Dickinson (Portsmouth), Matthews (Blackpool), Taylor (Blackpool), Mortensen (Blackpool), Sewell (Sheffield Wednesday), Robb (Tottenham Hotspur).

# "ENGLAND TO SLAM HUNGARY"

The Hungarian side was: Grosics; Buzanszky, Lantos, Bozsik, Lorant, Zakarias, Budai, Kocsis, Hidegkuti, Puskas, Czibor.

Ahead of the match there had not been overwhelming confidence in Hungary itself. Following their 1952 Olympic Games victory the players were almost immediately thrust back into League football, followed, in September, by an international against Switzerland in Berne. Sebes was anxious to resolve in his own mind whether he should play Palotas or Hidegkuti as the deep-lying centre forward. He decided to make Hidegkuti substitute but when Hungary conceded two goals in the first thirty minutes he took off Palotas and replaced him with Hidegkuti, who promptly created two goals for Puskas and seemed to have a natural understanding with Kocsis. Hungary won 4-2 and went on to beat Czechoslovakia 5-0. They finished the year unbeaten. Not only that, the problem of who should be the Number 9 had been solved in time for the visit to England.

When they arrived in London, Hungary had not suffered a defeat in three years. Among their victories had been a 3-0 win over Italy in Rome six months before the match against England. It was their first success over the Italians in twenty-eight years and contained plenty of useful information that should have been taken in by those who were supposed to be preparing England. The use of the teasing short pass, which encouraged defenders to move forward and out of position, and the accurate long one were the keys. In addition Hidegkuti was played in spite of not having recovered from an injury and scored once, with the other goals coming from Puskas. The style of play, with plenty of movement and accurate passing, was shrewdly planned by Sebes who, nevertheless, admitted that only on important occasions did he lecture the team on tactics. Generally speaking, in a tactical sense the players were left to their instincts, as had previous generations, all of whom had inherited the techniques originally taught by Hogan.

# PROPHET OR TRAITOR?

Then came a moment that Sebes believed could disrupt all of the preparations. In spite of today's massive publicity about players who drink to excess and make fools of themselves, there is nothing new about it. Sebes was told that less than three weeks before the match against England three of his players, Budai, Czibor and Kocsis, had left training one afternoon and spent the whole of the evening drinking at a nightclub. All were due to play in the imminent match against Czechoslovakia. The Hungarian newspapers got hold of the story and reported the incident in detail. Sebes decided that he had no choice but to omit the three from the game. Hungary still won with ease.

Sebes visited the players at their homes and discovered that Budai had actually returned to his home by midnight. The other two he warned as to their future conduct but said he wanted them to play against England. Both promised that they would never again cause him problems.

Sebes was meticulous in his personal preparation. He had visited England to see them scrape the draw against the Rest of Europe and deliberately took his football boots with him. He went back to Wembley on the afternoon after the game and got permission to try out the turf. He immediately realised that its softness meant that the ball did not bounce as much as on most pitches. He met Stanley Rous and asked whether he could borrow a ball similar to the one that would be used in the match itself. Rather over-generously, Rous gave him three, all of which he took back to Budapest. There he found a pitch that was nearly as soft as Wembley and the national squad trained on it for a fortnight before leaving for England. One of the squad, Buzanszky, admitted that when he first kicked one of the English footballs he thought it was made of wood.

Sebes had planned his reconnaissance trip to Wembley with such detail that he even made sure he was there soon after three o'clock to discover the exact position of the sun. It was Hogan who had first told him to be sure that he always took that into account.

Sebes was so pre-occupied with the game against England that he virtually overlooked a match against Sweden on November 15. He was probably over-confident since Hungary had easily beaten the Swedes in the Olympics. The match was played with one of the footballs Rous had provided but the Hungarians found it tricky to control. Also it was obvious that none of the side wanted to take risks so soon before the more important confrontation with England. They managed a draw but the Hungarian Press was damning. To a man the writers said the Hungarians had no chance against the English.

It was decided that the team needed to spend even more time together and have a moderately competitive practice match. Sebes arranged for them to stop in Paris on their way to London and play against a factory team. Not surprisingly the Hungarians scored thirteen goals, but it was a good boost for the spirits.

In London they stayed at the Cumberland Hotel. Sebes again planned everything down to the last detail, including the menus (something else he knew Hogan always liked to do). Since Rous realised he had been a shade over-polite in giving Sebes the footballs, he was not as keen to let the Hungarians train at Wembley so they had to use Loftus Road, the home of Queen's Park Rangers.

In spite of his insistence that he was not in favour of long tactical talks, Sebes knew that he was about to give the most significant one of his life. Primarily he was concerned about the strength of the English defence. In the game against Italy, he had encouraged his attackers and half backs to employ neat, short passes. Against England he wanted to see more possession and a great deal more running into space. It was almost as if Hogan was looking over his shoulder. In effect, he was asking for Total Football in which everyone would be free to make as much of the available space as possible and not be restricted to original positions. He particularly asked the wingers, Budai and Czibor, to remember that they could not relinquish their responsibilities when the ball was in their own half. He insisted that they tracked back to help in the middle of the field and defence. In other words they performed much in the style of today's wide midfield players. Above all, the team needed to rely on thoughtful links between the defenders and forwards.

Defensively, he played the sturdy Lorant as a stopper, though he was flexible enough to make the position more a variant of a sweeper. Buzanszky and Lantos were the two full backs and Zakarias was to be a midfield player with wide responsibilities, mainly as reliable cover for the defence but always ready to move forward in support of Bozsik and Hidegkuti. Sebes believed Bozsik, who had known Puskas from childhood and had played in the same Kispest club team, could be the game's most important player since he could slip forward into scoring positions while Hidegkuti, Puskas and Kocsis would whirl around in attack, causing England as much confusion as possible. The theory was that they could act as decoys, dragging the English defenders out of position like magnets. Puskas, even then more than a little chubby but instinctively quick off the mark, and Kocsis, slim and more thoughtful, made an interesting contrast in appearance and styles.

The Hungarian players listened to Sebes rambling on for a couple of hours and left the meeting feeling confused. Few of them were elevated by the theory and all admitted that on the morning of the game they felt more apprehensive than confident. Sebes reduced his match-day briefing to a few words which infused little further confidence in the team. The Hungarian News and Information Service reporter, who travelled with the party, gave a revealing view of the team's concern about the match and what happened in the hours before:

# "ENGLAND TO SLAM HUNGARY"

"25 November was an ordinary sort of day in London. Early in the morning a dense fog still enveloped the trees of Hyde Park, but when around 9 o'clock the Hungarian players began to assemble in the hall of the Cumberland Hotel, the porter said by way of encouragement: 'The fog will have cleared up completely by the time the game starts. As a matter of fact a bit of sunshine is expected.' The boys were gratified to hear this weather forecast, for on the previous evening a heavy rainfall had drenched the London streets and there were some whose nerves were so ruffled by the bad weather that they hardly slept a wink during the night.

"The greatest event in the hours just before a game is the tactical conference. The ponderings of long months, daring plans and novel ideas that are the fruits of many sleepless nights were given expression in the words of Gusztav Sebes at this tactical conference. 'England are great opponents but they can be defeated,' were his first words at the conference. He did not say much, so as not to tire the players. 'You, Nandi Hidegkuti, will begin playing as an advanced centre forward. This will confuse the English, who think that you will withdraw immediately. After the first minutes you will really play as a withdrawn centre-forward, but you will constantly change your position'. Then he explained in detail the tasks of the two wing-forwards: 'Budai and Czibor, your jobs won't be easy. You will have to play the entire length of the field and frequently you will have to meet the two English outside-forwards when they attack into our penalty area'. Then the leader of the Hungarian team turns to Bozsik: 'You are a key man. The English will pay less attention to you than our forwards. Make every effort to break through the gaps and shoot for goal, but defence is an important part of your task'. And Bozsik, a soft-spoken, modest sportsman, nodded his head in approval: 'That's how it will be, Uncle Guszti'.

# PROPHET OR TRAITOR?

"At 12.45, two policemen with motor-cycles arrived to escort the bus to Wembley Stadium. Once at the stadium, there was still an hour before the game. On other occasions they would have used this time to inspect the field and get acquainted with the spectators. But this time it was different. Everybody hurried to the dressing room and, without speaking, quietly began to change. When the English managers invited them to take a little walk out on the field Jozsef Zakarias remarked with grim humour: 'Who's interested in seeing the operating theatre before the operation?' Everyone was greatly pleased by the appearance in the dressing room of Gyula Hegyi, chairman of the National Committee for Physical Training and Sport, who was on his way to Chile with the Hungarian team for the modern pentathlon world championship, and interrupted his journey to see the game.

"The stands were already filled to capacity. The crowd was listening to the music of the Royal Air Force band, or looking over their official programmes. Finally, the referee's whistle was heard. The members of both teams marched on to the field.

"What will happen in London? Who will be the winner? Will the English be able to preserve their record of no home defeats? In Hungary, in the factories, co-operative farms and shops, the schools, the trams and restaurants, the England-Hungary match was the main topic of conversation. Everybody talked about the London weather, the ball, the dimensions of the field, about Puskas and the blond Wright, about Grosics and the reckless Merrick, about Bozsik and the lightning-swift Sewell, and about Lorant and the lion-hearted Mortensen with as much learning as the oldest football fans. Young and old, little boys and grandfathers, little girls and grandmothers - who have probably never seen a football match in their lives - were all in the greatest excitement over the England-Hungary game.

"It is not exaggeration to say that on the day of the great match the entire country awaited the news from London with

# "ENGLAND TO SLAM HUNGARY"

keen interest and excitement. The electrical shops did hurried business in the loaning of loudspeakers, amplifiers and radios. In the window of department stores, restaurants and shops notices were displayed: 'We are broadcasting the match of the century'. All over Budapest electricians busily installed loudspeakers. People besieged the offices of newspapers. 'How is the weather in London?'. 'Have any of the boys been injured?'. 'Is it true that there is a dense fog in London?'.

"Around 3 o'clock in the afternoon people were to be seen hurrying about. They were rushing to get home, or to a place where the match was being broadcast. By a quarter past three Budapest seemed deserted; only at a few places were there to be seen crowds where people had gathered round loudspeakers. The cinemas were showing films to almost empty houses; in the trams the crowding stopped during this otherwise busy hour and there were no passengers on the buses either. In many of the factories, at the request of the workers, the shift was begun earlier than usual."

Although the Hungarians may have been reluctant to go out on the pitch to warm up, they had spent half an hour preparing almost unnoticed on the grass outside the stadium where the greyhounds were kept. Among a few fascinated spectators was Malcolm Allison who was to become one of British football's most colourful, controversial yet exciting coaches. He went to Wembley early with Jimmy Andrews and... "I noticed their light, modern gear and their streamlined boots and that registered with me vaguely. But Jimmy pointed out the 'pot' bulging from the red shirt of No.10, Ferenc Puskas. 'God, we'll murder this lot', he said. You had to agree, even though there was a neatness and skill about their limbering. Then, out on the pitch just before the kick-off, I saw the 'fat guy' volleying shots into the arms of goalkeeper Grocics from forty yards. I said to Jimmy, 'They've got some skill, you know, it could be interesting."

# PROPHET OR TRAITOR?

The Hungarian players claimed that they knew little about the English side, and indeed none had ever been to England before, their homework had been more diligent than that of England who quickly regretted it. But, of course, the Hungarians were aware of the danger posed by Stanley Matthews, albeit at the age of thirty-eight, and the defensive organisational work of Wright. They were prepared to accept that Matthews might cause them problems on the wing but saw Wright as a great danger to their possession game. If they could deprive Wright of the ball they felt sure they could gain control of the match. Wright led out his team alongside Puskas. The home crowd smirked at the Hungarians short shorts and lightweight boots. But from the moment the men in red and white began to warm up, not flexing their muscles but performing little cameos of ball control, the smirks began to turn to frowns. Puskas went to the centre circle and flicked up the ball, juggling with it for a few moments…long enough to catch the eyes of the England players and scatter the first seeds of real doubt about the outcome.

From the moment the referee, Leo Horn, from Holland, blew the first whistle England were aware that they were about to face the biggest examination they or any of their predecessors had ever endured on home soil. Back in Budapest it was as if some alien craft had come and abducted everyone in sight. From the kick-off the ball went out of play. Hungary took the throw. Suddenly the confusion that Sebes wanted to see in the eyes of the English players was almost visible from his seat tens of yards away. Passes swept across the field, past the blank faces of the English defenders. Hidegkuti was impossible to interrupt. He exchanged passes with Bozsik, feinted, sidestepped Harry Johnston (who was playing his last international), took command of the space he himself had created then shot past Merrick. England were a goal down and had hardly come in contact with the ball.

# "ENGLAND TO SLAM HUNGARY"

The kingpin was Hidegkuti. He wore number nine but, as always, operated from behind the attack. England badly needed to get someone, anyone, to close mark him. No such instruction came from Walter Winterbottom, on the bench, or Wright who was in the middle of the emerging fiasco. Lantos admitted that he was mystified by Matthews's dribbling but later Matthews himself recalled that there always seemed to be one more defender to beat and, in any case, he felt isolated from the match and lacking confidence. He became frustrated by the fact that Hidegkuti seemed to be given total freedom.

Matthews yelled at Wright to get someone to close mark the rampaging Hidegkuti. Johnston was the obvious choice but by his own admission he was "utterly helpless" to stop the gathering clouds of despair and when at half-time Winterbottom asked him whether he wanted to mark Hidegkuti or defend generally, understandably he opted for the latter, believing that if he attempted a man-marking job England would be even more vulnerable to the counter-attacking. He commented later: "We would have done better if we had appointed one of the other players to mark Hidegkuti. Instead we all ended up marking space." Some time in the future Winterbottom admitted that he had never been in favour of going into the dressing room at half-time and criticising the players and, in spite of the situation, this was not to be an exception. Before that, however, the situation had got worse.

Wright had enough problems of his own without having time to worry about tactical changes. Like Johnston, he recalled "...we seemed to be marking the places they had just left." Yet after fifteen minutes the crowd got the impression that England had got to grips with their difficulties. Johnston made an interception in the England penalty area and sent a timely pass through for Mortensen to chase. Sewell went with him but pulled away into a gap. The Hungarians made the mistake of anticipating a shot from Mortensen who instead turned the ball towards Sewell, who thundered in a left-foot equaliser.

The Hungarian response was breathtaking. Puskas was the conductor and the home crowd had to watch the score become more and more irretrievable. He orchestrated move after move. He sent Czibor tearing down the left side. Kocsis flicked a pass to Hidegkuti who beat Merrick from close range off Eckersley, who was lunging hopelessly to stop the Hungarians taking the lead. Czibor's speed was a major problem. Again he tore away down the right edge in pursuit of Kocsis' pass. And again Eckersley was left fuming as he failed to intercept. Kocsis's crossed the ball to Puskas who conjured one of the greatest goals ever seen at Wembley. First he had to avoid Wright, which he did by dragging the ball back with the sole of his boot (shades of Hogan's coaching) leaving the England captain tackling thin air. Almost instantaneously he drove a fierce left foot shot into the net. The audacity, simplicity and artistry of the goal was unforgettable. Modestly, Puskas later said that far from his drag back being something he had rehearsed time and again, it was in reality an instant decision that he hoped would avoid his being smothered by Wright's tackle. Nevertheless, to achieve it was remarkable.

Probably more than anyone Wright, the proud leader, felt that as the game slipped away he should have been able to do more to prepare his team for the challenge. He was not ready for the quality of the Hungarians and he concluded that Hogan was right. English football had stagnated. One evening in the Seventies, after watching yet another less than subtle display by an England side at Wembley, he said: "I don't think that we had ever been prepared to look at what the foreign sides had done and been ready to think that they could teach us something. The Hungarians were the first to show us how to play collectively. You thought each player knew exactly what the other would do without waiting to see it happen. After we

# "ENGLAND TO SLAM HUNGARY"

lost at Wembley most of the players realised that we had a lot of work to do, but even after we were slaughtered in Budapest people were still saying that it was just something that would soon be forgotten because we had the best league in the world."

Before even half an hour of the game at Wembley had gone, Hungary were 4-1 ahead. Bozsik played a free-kick into the penalty area and Puskas's heel diverted it in as Merrick made a forlorn dive across goal. Matthews and Mortensen desperately tried to inject England's performance with the spirit that earlier in the year Blackpool had shown on the same pitch. Robb revealed a similar defiance with a fine header that Grosics managed to save, but not easily. Then Mortensen went on a long run which, unusually, was not seriously challenged. He broke into the penalty area and beat Grosics. As the half-time whistle sounded, England knew they were being outplayed but at least they had made a play for a comeback.

From the moment he took the job Winterbottom had been convinced that his work would be severely restricted by having an FA sub committee still select the team and his own time with the players limited. It was showing. Sebes had been working with his group much more frequently.

Ten minutes into the second half Geoffrey Green was faced with the moral dilemma that Hogan himself was feeling as he watched from his position near the Press box. Green was fiercely patriotic yet his professional pride was being flattered by events out there on the pitch. Everything he had predicted was coming true. The same could be said of Hogan. England were putting every possible effort into avoiding being humiliated but it was inevitable. It had given Green no satisfaction to write what he, and Hogan, had thought obvious. The Continent had not only caught up but here in Fortress Wembley, shortly after half-time, he scrawled in his notebook "the past is dead and buried for ever". As always, he sat making an occasional note, remembering every detail and at the end he dictated to The Times, more or less ad lib, the most historically significant football report of his life. The second half of the game simply confirmed his prediction.

Merrick, shaken in the England goal, was all too aware that he could be made the scapegoat for England's rising defeat. But this was a day when he came up against the unstoppable. He managed to turn a header from Czibor on to the post but the Hungarians came at him in a wave of red shirts. Bozsik crashed in Hungary's fifth. Puskas then lobbed a pass to Hidegkuti who volleyed in the sixth. There were thirty minutes left when Mortensen was brought down and Ramsey scored from the penalty spot. It would not have mattered if England had been favoured with an hour. There was no way that they could recover, and to rub salt in the wound, ten minutes from the end Hungary's goalkeeper Grosics, who played in three World Cups and achieved eighty-nine caps in his remarkable career, went off with an arm injury and was replaced by Geller. In his inimitable style, Green recorded: "By now a Hungarian goalkeeper was but a formal requirement".

Hidegkuti had not only been the most inspirational player of the match but led the way to a succession of effective strikers who would drop deep to cause defences to move out and leave space. Among those who followed him were Don Revie and, in later years, as an example, Teddy Sheringham. Hidegkuti's career, which had begun with two small clubs, Elektromos and Herminanzero, brought him an Olympic gold medal but not the World Cup gold his talents deserved. He retired after the 1958 World Cup to take up management work in Italy. He guided Fiorentina to victory in the first European Cup Winners' Cup final, against Rangers in 1961. When he returned to Hungary in 1963, remarkably he coached a comparatively small club, Gyori ETO, to the league championship and took them to the semi-final of the European Cup. His career finished in Egypt where he worked with the Al-Ahly club that won five league titles.

# "ENGLAND TO SLAM HUNGARY"

Looking back at the Wembley match, one could say that none of the England players was individually seriously at fault, not even Merrick, who had experienced better days. The fault was with the English game itself and with the failure of the selectors to do their homework. Hungary had been playing with a deep lying centre forward long enough for any moderately astute coach to work out a way in which the system could, at least, be hindered. Instead, the England players were not even warned. Green ended his report by saying "English football can be proud of its past. But it must awake to a new future".

The man upon whom fell the responsibility of rousing the English game was still Winterbottom, who was understood better by the members of the Press than he was by the average player. He was a kindly, intelligent man who was rightly credited with forcing the FA to realise that English football desperately needed to place much greater emphasis on coaching. For his first seven years as "manager" he was never allowed to manage. And when he was faced with the fact that English football was no longer in the forefront of the game internationally, but a whole generation behind, it was too late. Unlike his successor, Alf Ramsey, he was not practical enough to look at the strengths of the English game and create a team that would make it difficult for other sides to operate. That was not the way he felt football should be played. He shared that sentiment with Hogan.

Ramsey himself was deeply hurt by being a part of the 1953 defeat and believed that the outcome could have been avoided. Long after he had become England's manager he would say that had the Hungarians been denied possession in the middle of the field, the result would have been different. As if suggesting that a few tactical changes could have denied the fact that English football was at last being made to face reality, he said that most of the goals came from outside the penalty area. What he failed to admit was that it was in exactly that area that England were completely outclassed. Generously, Bozsik told Geoffrey Green that England in his eyes were and would remain the "masters" but he also said that without Hogan's work in his country "in the early years of learning" the possibility of such a victory would not have arisen.

All of the England players were stunned by the quality of the Hungarians' football. Wright said it was a game in which he always felt England were attempting to catch up with many seasons of neglect. He denied that these particular England players were not prepared mentally, saying that Winterbottom had seen Hungary play and warned that it would not be an easy match. But he confessed that in all of his career he had never come across a more complete team. Stanley Matthews agreed; "The best team I ever played against because every player had such skill".

Peter McParland, who having been among the Villa youngsters Hogan had taken to Wembley, agreed entirely with Matthews's assessment. He said: "This was the best team I had ever seen and have ever seen play football. You can talk about the 1970 Brazilian team but this was better than that. I was sitting with Jimmy and Vic Crowe and when the Hungarians kicked off and kept passing the ball I said 'Here we go, all possession and no shots'. Then, it seemed within seconds, Hidegkuti dropped his shoulder and Harry Johnston bought it. Hidegkuti let fly and from then on it was a joy to watch. The people from Hungary dedicated the match to Jimmy because he had shown them that this was the way he wanted them to play. England just didn't know what to do. They were up against two very fast wingers and Hidegkuti was causing damage all the time. England couldn't get contact with the ball but Hungary also had big hard men at the back."

McParland remembered that when he and the other junior players returned to Birmingham the next day and started training again with Hogan, their respect had heightened. "He got us involved in the things that players do today: getting us to work together. I believe that Jimmy could have been used at a national level after the game at Wembley. Walter Winterbottom had good ideas about coaching but Jimmy could have gone into that and set it up as an adviser. He could have advanced the game a great deal. It's amazing to think that we had a man like that at our fingertips and we didn't grab him back in the Thirties. Even when I was a boy in Ireland, I saw Norway and Finland come to Dublin and their possession was great. Then the Swedish team that won the Olympics under George Raynor ran the Irish side to bits in Dublin."

While British players who thought they were too superior to require coaching often dismissed Hogan as being something of an eccentric, or at least too old to have anything useful to say, the Villa youngsters were won over by someone who treated them as adults yet at the same time had a fatherly attitude. McParland had a particular reason to be grateful for Hogan's arm of protection. By 1957 he had become an established member of the first team who won their way to the FA Cup Final against Manchester United's "Busby Babes". Several previous finals had been ruined by injuries. In 1952 Arsenal's Wally Barnes had to go off with a knee injury. In 1953 Eric Bell, of Bolton, retired from the Final with a badly pulled muscle. The following year Manchester City's Jimmy Meadows had to abandon.

On the day before the 1957 Final members of the Football Association discussed whether or not it was time to introduce substitutes, but decided against it. The following day they were ridiculed as another Final was affected by an injury. McParland and United's goalkeeper, Ray Wood, collided. "A lot of people still say that I bundled him into the net, but that incident was the following year and it was Harry Gregg. We collided in the penalty area," McParland remembered, "and we both went down. When I came round the stadium was going round and round." McParland recovered but Wood, who after they both retired became a good friend and golf partner, had to play on the wing. Villa won the match 2-1 with McParland scoring both goals and, unfairly, becoming reviled by United supporters.

"After a few days I began to get the hate mail," McParland said. "It became a big pile but someone said 'Here, give that to me'. That was old Jimmy who sifted it all out. He showed it to the manager, Eric Houghton, but made sure I didn't see any of it. That was something he would, in a way, have enjoyed - looking after you." In the following season the clubs made up their differences when Houghton and Matt Busby agreed to make McParland and Wood captains for the day at the Charity Shield.

McParland vouched for Hogan's massive influence on players abroad. He explained: "We had played the Germans in a World Cup qualifying match in Belfast in 1960 and had been leading 2-1 but lost 4-3. On the next day we are flying back from Belfast to Manchester and the German team are on the same plane. I was sitting back when Helmut Schoen, who was the assistant manager to Sepp Herberger, came along and sits next to me and he says 'Do you know where Jimmy Hogan is?'. I said I'm going back so I'll see him tomorrow in Birmingham. So Helmut says 'Right' and gets some paper out and writes a whole big letter to Jimmy and gave it to me. Then the President of the German Federation came along and he also wrote out a note to Jimmy. Helmut told me he was one of Jimmy's players and that he was a great man." Schoen had been with Dresden when Hogan was their coach.

Among the spectators at Wembley was also the Wolves manager, Stan Cullis, who was fascinated by the fact that the Hungarians could play a long ball game almost as accurately as the short. He was sceptical about the possession play that had so impressed the spectators and most of the writers. He said it

# "ENGLAND TO SLAM HUNGARY"

was only made possible because of the substantial lead that Hungary took and upon which they could play keep-ball. He seemed to ignore the fact that Hungary had to win their domination in the first place and against players for whom they had high respect. The long ball game was simply a small part of their considerable repertoire.

It would be churlish to criticise Cullis, whose fine club side scored over 100 goals in four successive seasons and beat the fading Honved, but he became a follower of Wing Commander Reep, an accountant officer in the RAF who reduced football to statistical analysis which, according to him, proved that the long ball sent more in hope than promise was always more likely to produce a goal than any imaginative work done by skillful players in midfield. Brazil, Holland and France, amongst others of recent years, seem to have proved the opposite. All have utilised long passing but caringly and when the opportunity was appropriate.

The following morning, when, incidentally, Stanley Rous took half of the game's gate money to Hungary's hotel but was told that all he needed to do was promise a return game (in hindsight he might have saved further embarrassment by insisting that the Hungarians took the money and forgot about inviting England to play in Hungary), the telephone in Aston Villa manager Eric Houghton's office was bombarded with calls from the Press and any number of people who had come in contact with Hogan over the years, all either wanting to interview him or simply congratulate him on the work he had done to produce the sort of football they had seen the previous afternoon. Hogan himself was "unavailable", preferring to be out on the pitch with the youngsters who had been with him at Wembley. Meanwhile, the reporter with the Hungarian News and Information Service travelled back with the team and described their arrival at the first railway station after crossing the border back into their home country:

# PROPHET OR TRAITOR?

"Perhaps never in its history has the little frontier railway station in Hegyeshalom been as active as on the night of 2 and 3 December. Not only did the local residents stay up all night but many people of the surrounding region and even Budapest came to be the first to shake hands with the London victors. And truly this wonderful moment, when the train bearing the footballers pulled into Hegyeshalom and the Hungarian national anthem played, made everyone forget every bit of fatigue. 'Puskas! Bozsik! Kocsis!'. The names are shouted as the players appeared at the windows of the train. Their families, sporting friends and strangers hurried to the train that they may be able to speak to them as soon as possible. The train started on its way to Budapest. All along the waves of enthusiasm met the boys. In Gyor, Komarom, Tatabanya and wherever the train stopped, showers of flowers, gifts and recognition for their performance met the footballers. Everywhere the fans wanted to delay the train.

"On the train, the match was the only topic of conversation. The coaches and the leaders of the sports associations listened with great attention to the most minute details of the London match. Lorant described how the English players marked Puskas and how he was still able to shoot two goals. Zakarias praised the sportsmanlike English spectators who applauded the Hungarian goals just as much as those scored by the English players. Coach Gyula Mandi recalled how wonderfully the players adhered to instructions and how much the forwards moved about and even helped in the rear when necessary. There would have been much more to talk about, but the train was already in the outskirts of Budapest. And when it rolled into the glass-roofed building of the East Railway Terminus, the next few minutes were memorable. Tens of thousands of the capital's population greeted the players with boundless affection."

Several days later all of the squad, including the coaches, attended the Parliament building and received one of Hungary's greatest honours, the Order of Merit.

# "ENGLAND TO SLAM HUNGARY"

Amongst the conclusions reached by journalists in England was the notion that players in the national team were different from other nationals in that they considered domestic competition (the League and the FA Cup) to be the supreme test. International matches were just added on. No player who had, or has since, worn an England shirt would subscribe to such an excuse.

The matches against Hungary emphasised that world football had come to the crossroads and that England had clearly taken the wrong direction. Naturally the England selectors made several changes for the summer tour match against the Hungarians in Budapest, which was played ahead of the 1954 World Cup in Switzerland. Matthews, who, despite his own feeling of frustration at not being sufficiently involved, was the only player the Hungarians admitted had troubled them at Wembley. For the return game he was replaced by Tom Finney who was played on the left wing. Merrick retained his position in goal but with his confidence disturbed.

Hungary's 7-1 win could have been even worse. In the meantime, Winterbottom's plans for the improvement of coaching on a nationwide basis were still struggling through the approval process at the FA. Billy Wright admitted that little progress was made after the defeats at Wembley and in Budapest. He said that too many people simply ignored the "slaughter" in Hungary. England went on to be eliminated from the World Cup in the quarter-finals by Uruguay. Since Matthews and Finney, supposedly the greatest wingers in the world, both played, the excuses ran dry and Hogan's warnings became haunting whispers in the administrative corridors of English football.

# 19

# The Sadness

THE FOLLOWING YEAR, RECALLING the Wembley match, Hogan wrote in the magazine Sport: "Although I received numerous congratulations at the end of the game, I was very sad indeed. After all, I am a British coach - and during my twenty-one years' teaching experience of the Continent of Europe, I have always fought hard for the prestige of British football. Though I was thrilled to see my old pupils give such a grand display, it came as a shock to see England defeated. Football is a British game - and we taught the world how to play it. I still maintain that we have the best players, but it is our style of playing the game which has gone wrong - not forgetting our modern training methods which are seriously at fault."

To put the quality of the Hungarians into perspective, just consider their record between 1950 and 1956. In that period they lost only one of their forty-eight international matches and scored 210 goals. In addition they achieved an unbeaten home record that lasted for eleven years. It was built on careful coaching and making sure that they never fell for the modern managers' excuse for his own laziness in preparation: "We'll let the opposition worry about us". They studied the strengths and weaknesses of every opponent and always knew exactly what they were facing.

The Hungarians had been on the learning escalator since 1936 when they visited Highbury and were comfortably beaten

# THE SADNESS

6-2. They found themselves facing the "stopper" centre half system developed by Chapman while they allowed their own centre half to play in midfield. Ted Drake had gorged himself on the space he was allowed and scored three goals. Hungary felt humiliated, not because they had played badly (their individual control and work in midfield was quite as good as England's), but for having failed to respond to the new tactic. They even sent one of their association's coaching staff to England to spend nearly a year studying the "stopper" role.

Perhaps the first match to show their progress towards becoming the best team in the world had been one against Austria in 1945 when Puskas made his international debut. Victory included his first goal for his country. However, a 5-2 defeat by Czechoslovakia a year later forced the authorities into re-thinking the way international football had to be approached. They then gathered together a squad, rather than selecting randomly, and held them together for as long as possible. Puskas's army club, Honved, always contributed at least fifty per cent of the group. The retaining of team continuity as a policy began in the Forties and was rarely broken until the World Cup of 1954 when Puskas was injured and missed two matches before returning, not fully fit, for the final against West Germany. Czibor was asked to play on the right wing, Toth came in on the left and Budai was dropped. A 3-2 defeat left them in tears - understandably so. They had lost their first game in thirty and their period of seeming invincibility was almost over. Brazil were about to re-establish the superiority of South American football which Hogan had predicted.

Some indication of Hungary's quality can be gauged by the fact that in 1954 England were still good enough to beat Scotland 7-2. Tommy Docherty had the misfortune to play in that match and mused that it made him realise just what a fine team the Hungarians must have been to overwhelm England.

# PROPHET OR TRAITOR?

Later that year at Hampden Park he played against the Hungarians. Scotland lost 4-2. When Scotland then went to Budapest, they led 1-0 at half-time and were unfortunate to see Billy Liddell waste a penalty. They lost 3-1. Docherty said that more than anything else, he was impressed with the way the Hungarians dictated the pace of any game in which they played. Hogan had always maintained that the likely winners of any match would always be the one forcing the other side to do the chasing.

Docherty explained: "Their passing movements made us British footballers feel as if they had come to our pitches from another planet. They would lull you into a false sense of security with a procession of quick, short passes that took them nowhere and then suddenly unleash a paralysing long pass that would arrive in space a split-second ahead of one of their 'tuned-in' team mates. They more than any team I have ever seen realized the importance of supporting runs. Every time a player was in possession he would have a minimum of two and sometimes as many as five team-mates getting into positions where they could receive the ball. It made it a nightmare for we defenders trying to work out who to pick up."

Winterbottom returned from the 1954 World Cup to continue his debate with the FA about spending more time with his players. Up to a point he eventually got his way, having a say in the selection but it still had to be approved by full committee. Of equal importance was the acceptance by the FA that much more emphasis should be put on coaching. Hogan, who always felt that Winterbottom should have been given greater responsibility in order to prove whether or not he was the right man for the job, said it was too little too late.

Any interpretation of Winterbottom's career remains locked in ambiguity. Hogan hardly knew him and took a kindly but slightly questioning view simply because he was not what today would be called a "hands on" coach - one who could demonstrate everything he wanted to teach. Without doubt Winterbottom always worked under the dead hand of the FA's determination to keep control of the England side, but in spite of that he was the one who dictated the team's tactical approach to matches, not least against the Hungarians.

Had he been seriously concerned about the threatening changes taking place in the world game, he would have taken note that a month before the match at Wembley, Sweden, under the experienced guidance of Raynor, had gone to Budapest and managed a draw. Raynor had earlier watched the Hungarians and, in particular, noted the special skills of Hidegkuti. Unlike Winterbottom, he had that exceptional player marked man-to-man. Not only that, he had him marked by a different player in the second half. Hidegkuti ran out of steam, but without any doubt he, even more than his lifelong friend Puskas, was the single most influential player of the period and the one who most caught the imagination of the British public. He had been brought up to believe in the accurate short-passing game that Hogan had taught and had a similar background of learning. His education was the football of the streets and rough pitches.

For all of his ability as a director of coaching with the FA, Winterbottom was never a touchline screamer who could alter the course of events with an inspired and sudden change of tactics. Much as he appreciated the importance of complete ball control, he felt that by the time players got to work with him they should have been more than competent in that respect. He sometimes assumed too much. At an England training session, Len Shackleton sat and listened to Winterbottom. He was far from convinced, explaining later: "Before one match against Wales, Walter got out the blackboard and outlined exactly what he wanted done from the kick-off. 'Milburn will pass the ball back to Wright. He will play it wide to Finney. Milburn and Mortensen will make dummy runs into the penalty area but Finney will cut inside

# PROPHET OR TRAITOR?

and play it to Shackleton on the edge of the box, and Shackleton will kick it into the net.' I looked at him and said, 'Which side, Walter, left or right?' He was not amused, and although we beat Wales 4-1 I never played for England again for five years."

Shackleton was among those who in the aftermath of England's 1953 defeat suggested that it was not too late for Hogan to be used by the FA to restore the national team. In his book "Clown Prince of Soccer" he wrote: "It would be desirable to have a man at the top with Walter Winterbottom's grounding in theory, and the practical skill of a Peter Doherty. My ideal, and I had to do a lot of searching, would be Jimmy Hogan, the man who taught such nations as Hungary and Austria how to play football.

"Ageless Jimmy Hogan - people guess his age as anything between 65 and 75 - is the greatest coach football has ever known. For years he has been a 'wanted' man all over the world - except in his own country, England…that great football sage has been driven from pillar to post, proving once again what a tremendous struggle faces even the best coaches who try to make a living with League clubs in Britain.

"Come to think of it, I might still be an Arsenal player had the Gunners been blessed with a man like Jimmy Hogan to coach their younger players. The late Jack Lambert was in charge of the young Highbury lads when I was there, but despite his success as a goal-scoring centre forward - flanked on either side by David Jack and Alex James - he was not the ideal type of footballer for a responsible position as a coach to a great club. Even as a 16-year-old I imagine I had certain potentialities which might have been spotted by a David Jack, an Alex James or a Jimmy Hogan, although missed by Lambert."

In a way Winterbottom shared Hogan's misfortune. In Winterbottom's case the FA failed to see that he had the ability

210

# THE SADNESS

to become one of the game's most talented administrators. Sadly, when Rous moved on to become FIFA president Winterbottom was not offered the chance to be secretary of the Football Association. The position would not only have suited him well but he could have revitalised the English game.

After Winterbottom's death in 2002 David Lacey, The Guardian's ever-discerning Football Correspondent, wrote: "As a teacher of those who would eventually do the teaching, his influence on the coaching side of English football was more profound than anything he achieved as the original manager of the England team." Lacey pointed out that Winterbottom was only forty-nine when he left the FA to become general secretary of the Central Council for Physical Recreation and, needlessly, was lost to football at an early age. He wrote: "The answer is FA politics, or rather the petty attitudes which prevailed at Lancaster Gate in the early '60s and for a long time after. When Stanley Rous, the lordly secretary of the FA, left to become president of FIFA it was assumed Winterbottom would succeed him. But the council chose Denis Follows by a 50-20 vote, plumping, in Rous's words, "for the good at the expense of the excellent".

Lacey concluded: "Had Winterbottom become the FA's chief administrator, the chain of events, and non-events, which led to the country appointing a foreign coach because suitable English candidates were no longer around might have been avoided." Winterbottom's record in international football was not at all bad. His England teams played 136 matches and had seventy-six wins and twenty eight defeats. The only problem was that the defeats too often came on the big occasions. Only three out of fourteen World Cup matches were won and in 1950 and 1958 England were eliminated in the first round, while in 1954 and 1962 they got only as far as the quarter finals. Against that, it has to be mentioned that he lost several fine players in the Munich air crash and earlier had seen others move to South America for what at the time were high financial rewards.

# PROPHET OR TRAITOR?

While the Hungarians generously praised Hogan for laying the foundations of their wonderful football, the fact is that they ought to have been linking his name with that of another Englishman, Arthur Rowe, who spent only five weeks in Budapest at the invitation of the Central Committee of Sport early in 1940 but made a big impression. Like Hogan, he lectured and demonstrated. Because of what he told them about the game in Britain, they realised that they had to adapt themselves to the third-back game. Rowe went on to manage the outstanding "push and run" Tottenham teams of the early 1950s. When Gustav Sebes took over the Hungarian national team and developed the style of play that so astounded people in Britain, his first priority was to follow what Rowe had advised by adapting the third-back game so that it was not predominantly defensive.

After England's humiliation prestige at home badly needed to be raised and was done so, rather misleadingly, by Stan Cullis's Wolves side who in the winter of 1954 took on first Spartak Moscow and then Puskas's Honved. There is no doubt that both matches were full of excitement and had the country enthralled. These were the early days of efficient floodlit football and the matches became both theatre and sport. Spartak held Wolves, captained by Billy Wright, to 0-0 until the 80th minute when the home team's fitness (based on Cullis's tough training routines) came to their rescue and they scored four goals.

The reaction was understandable but over-blown. There were even suggestions that the whole of the England team should be replaced by the one from the Wolverhampton club. Some critics were slightly more cautious and waited to see how Honved performed. More than anyone, Wright wanted some compensation for his England team's embarrassments the previous year. Wright and Puskas were to become close friends but not on December 13, 1954.

# THE SADNESS

Honved included five of the team that had played in that year's World Cup final. In a thrilling match, initially they showed the sort of Hogan-generated football that the Hungarians had cultivated so successfully, but the enormous spirit and overwhelming atmosphere created by the crowd swung the game back towards Wolves, who won 3-2. The victory on a rain-soaked, muddy pitch that grasped and devalued the ball players was portrayed as complete a vindication of English football's standing in the world. In reality, Honved were a weary team and looked upon the game less seriously than Wolves who, when they were later put to the real test of European Cup football, were found wanting against the skills of, amongst others, Barcelona and Real Madrid. In the 1958-59 season they were knocked out by Dukla Prague in the second round, in 1959-60 they beat ASK Vorwarts of Berlin, and Red Star Belgrade, but were easily swept aside 9-2 on aggregate by Barcelona.

Although Cullis had grandly described his team as "champions of the world", Willy Meisl made the point that not long before the game at Molineux, Honved had lost 3-2 away to Red Star Belgrade "and no-one called Red Star champions of the world". Even so, the remark by Cullis was defiant and thought-provoking enough to be the spur that led to the founding of the European Cup.

The lads Hogan had taken to Wembley were highly impressed not only with the Hungarians but because of the old man's prediction that they would see something they would never forget. Those who saw him perform his stage demonstrations at town and village halls also never forgot that he could always practice what he preached. One of his grandsons, Chris Riding, recalled that he was regularly asked to take part. "Grandad would get me and some local players up there and would demonstrate trapping and passing, but then he would often get me to stand legs apart at one side of the stage and he would be at the other and hit footballs between my legs - I didn't even think of protecting myself like today's players do at free-kicks. I had complete confidence in him. He never seemed to make a mistake. Well, not quite never."

Hogan often coached at schools and as old age crept on he was not always able to display the fine ball control that he insisted was the essence of the game. On one visit his old skills momentarily vanished. One of the pupils, Jim Pollard, recalled that Hogan had "tried to demonstrate corner kicking to the class in the assembly hall because in those days there were no areas outside on which to play, and he managed to put the ball through the glass partition of the classroom". More often than not, though, his accuracy remained impressive. John Whittaker remembered him coming to his school. "As well as talking to us, he gave some demonstrations. At one point he got about ten footballs. He chipped them into a bucket as soon as we could fetch them out."

When asking youngsters to try their hand, he was always searching for potential professionals. So what exactly did he look for when attempting to discover exceptional young players? He once remarked that the most important thing was "intelligence". He explained: "He may not be having a very good game but then he does something which tells me that he has a good football brain. No, it can't be done unless a boy has a football brain."

John Gleeson, who was a pupil at St. Mary's School, Burnley in the early Fifties was taught by Jimmy's sister, Kate, who lived in Todmorden Road. He recalled: "On this particular day in 1952 an immaculately dressed man in blazer and flannels was introduced to our class as her brother James. Presumably he had been induced by her to come to the school to meet the boys and give a talk on his football experiences and perhaps give a coaching lesson. At this time we had no idea who he was.

# THE SADNESS

"He held us enthralled as he chatted about football and coaching in England and Europe, including his time in Hungary years before. He told us about the philosophy that had seen English football paramount throughout the world as inventors of the game, and its masters. We were instructed by this man into another dimension on tactics and strategy both verbally and on the blackboard. It was riveting stuff and we were a spellbound schoolboy audience. No class was ever more attentive and captivated. He drew and explained triangular movements on the blackboard...pass and move...pass the ball and move into the open space for the return...evade the crunching tackles while defenders were still ball watching...the advantage of the short corner to keep possession and draw tall defenders out of the penalty area...short free-kicks to keep momentum and prevent the opposition getting back...goalkeepers to throw the ball out to a team-mate rather than see goalkicks inevitably kicked straight back by the opposition's big centre half. Pass your way through defenders...get behind the ball when defending."

Apart from coaching and advising youngsters, another of Hogan's favourite pursuits was blasting off letters to the Press about the state of the game and interfering club chairmen and directors. In one he wrote: "Our former intelligent ideas are gradually fading out. We have developed an up-in-the-air, get-the-ball-if-you-can game. We are continuously kicking the ball down the middle to the marked centre forward. Fifty years ago when I was at school I was taught that to pass the ball to a man who was covered was a grave error.

"Englishmen are not exploiting the effective wing game as they used to do. This is, incidentally, the best manner of opening out the opponent's defence. Instead of creating openings by playing constructive football we are often booting the ball aimlessly down the field in the hope of opponents making a defensive error which would result in a goal-scoring

215

chance. In tackling the third-back game we send up three forwards with the two inside men generally well in the rear. Just think of it.

"I have been told that this generation demands speed and thrills. Well, we can cater for them in this respect and still play football in an intelligent manner. I do not blame the football player - he has to play to orders. I blame the interfering gentlemen who have the habit of walking into dressing rooms. Many do not possess the foggiest notion of the game, but nevertheless are continuously whispering into players' ears: 'Get stuck in'." He concluded, however, by saying that he still believed that few Continental players could compete with British ones in terms of natural ability, but he doubted whether, because of outdated coaching and tactics with which he so vehemently disagreed, the contemporary ones had the right background to return England to a position of important strength in the world game.

Many other boys who were taught by Hogan have clear memories of the impression he made on them. Peter Ogden, of Colne, who attended St. Bede's College, recalled: "One day in the mid-Fifties, when Mr. Hogan would have been well over seventy years of age, we had the privilege of receiving a soccer coaching session from him in the school gymnasium. To us as young boys he seemed positively ancient and we were amazed when he took off his shoes and socks, rolled up his trouser legs and proceeded to show us how to kick a football properly.

"I flinched as his foot hit the ball, expecting him to hear a cry of pain from him. Instead we were aghast as he hammered the unsuspecting football with tremendous force against the wall-bars: incredibly, it seemed, for such a venerable gentleman who could have been someone's grandfather." Ogden stored away a copy of the school magazine of the time in which it reported: "We had a welcome visit from Jimmy Hogan, an old boy of the College. He is in the best of form and enlivened the break of the staff with stories of religious strife in Glasgow."

Hogan's fame abroad was lasting. Denis Guilfoyle, whose mother was Jimmy's sister, stayed with the family in Paris for nine months in 1931-32 when he ghosted a number of newspaper articles for his uncle who often dabbled in journalism. Recalling that while in Hungary Jimmy was known as "Jimmy Bacsi", he said: "Hungarian visitors to the house in Paris always used the expression Bacsi and many years later, at an international convention organised by United Steel in Sheffield, I was seated at dinner with an Hungarian delegation. I asked one of them if he had known 'Jimmy Bacsi' and he lit up. 'Mr. Hogan, you know him,' he said. I explained the relationship, saying that I had spent the previous Sunday with him. He wrote out a postcard for me to give to Uncle Jimmy, which said: 'Dear Mr.Hogan. Here is your wonderful MTK team of 1912' (and he listed the players). With all my regards, Gyeorgi .....' I can't remember his surname."

Others have good reason to remember the name of Hogan, not always because he coached them or even encouraged them. Indeed, when he heard that Hogan's story was to be published Mr. A. Cheetham, of Burnley, was one of the first to write offering some memories of meeting with the old man who probably saved him from becoming one of football's many disappointed hopefuls. Shortly before the outbreak of the Second World War he was determined to become a professional player. He said: "I was an apprentice electrician at the time but had quite a name as a 16-year-old local player in the Sunday School league. I had a couple of run-outs with the Burnley 'A' but it led to nothing. I tried Nelson who were then playing in the Lancashire Combination, which was a high class league that would compare with today's Conference. Youngsters left for the big league and there were old pros who had stepped down.

# PROPHET OR TRAITOR?

"Training at Nelson's ground, Seedhill, I was intrigued by the interest shown in me by a guy who was giving me close scrutiny. I must confess I was a little flattered and asked someone who he was. I was told 'Jimmy Hogan' but mistaking an 'o' for an 'a', due to the bloke's Geordie accent, I thought he meant Jimmy Hagan, the great Sheffield United inside left. 'No, you daft bugger, it's Jimmy Hogan the famous coach…he's a local lad.'

"Mr. Hogan then gave me some good advice by telling me I would need to be a little better to be a pro. When I told him my job he said 'Play amateur football and enjoy it - there's a war coming. You'd be better off being an electrician'. I think his experience in Austria told him that war was inevitable. He asked about a big plaster I had on my forehead. I told him I got it playing cricket. I found he had a great love of the game.

"Six years war service in the RAF would have meant that when I came out I would have been twenty-four so there was not much chance of making it in pro-soccer. So you might say that his wise words altered my life for the better. He also made a lasting impression on me by the way he talked personally to me. I was reminiscing with a young airman in a tent in Egypt during the war. It turned out he was a colt at a northern team and I talked about Mr. Hogan. The young man later captained a first division club so I had better not name him, but he said that Jimmy Hogan was the worst thing ever for English and Scottish soccer."

By the mid-Seventies the Hungarians had to accept that the expressive, attractive and highly skilled football of the Fifties was no longer as likely to bring rewards. The game had changed again, becoming much quicker, with defenders challenging attackers at similar pace. Players of Puskas's era were undoubtedly given far more time on the ball. Lajos Baroti took them to the World Cup final competitions of 1958, 1962 and 1966, but all the time he was becoming more and more

# THE SADNESS

aware that Hungary's natural flair was being questioned. In the end he came up with a compromise style embracing dedicated practice in the skills of the game while at the same time improving stamina and ensuring that training included far more work in competitive situations.

Whereas in the Fifties players would spend hours developing their ball control but only faced being tackled in actual matches, Baroti insisted on hard practice games. Hogan would probably have disapproved and as the Swinging Sixties approached he decided that the world had changed and so had football. So in 1959, at the age of 77, he finally gave up his close links with the game, left Birmingham and again went back to live in Burnley. Yet he still kept in touch with Villa and often called them when he spotted a promising local player. He would rather have tipped off Burnley but it was Villa who still provided a pension.

He continued to pay the occasional visit to Seedhill to watch Nelson, and in September, 1960 a journalist on the local newspaper, Eric Greenwood, followed up one of his visits and went to see him at his home. He described Hogan as a "dapper, agile and most amiable Gentleman of Sport who looked much younger than he was". Hogan told him: "I have been soccer daft ever since I was a young boy, and I always will be."

Looking back on his career, Hogan wrote: "When I studied geography as a boy at school, and read about the Land of the Midnight Sun, Sunny Italy and Spain, the blue Mediterranean, the Black Forest, the wonderful Swiss Mountains, the charming cities of Budapest, Vienna, Berlin, Paris, Rome, Copenhagen, Stockholm, Barcelona and so on, there always came an eternal longing in my breast. I often gazed at the map of Europe and thought to myself how happy I would be if I only had the opportunity of visiting those wonderful places abroad.

"Little did I think in those happy boyhood days - when I was kicking the big ball on Gannow Top Recreation Ground -

that football would be the means of satisfying my craving for visiting strange lands and people; but it came to pass. My dreams have been realised."

In 1962, when he celebrated his 80th birthday, he was living with his niece, Margaret Melia, in Brunshaw Avenue, close to his beloved Turf Moor. Messages of congratulations came from all over the world. He remarked that had he been just a few years younger he might have applied for the England manager's job in succession to Winterbottom. He added that if he had his way it would be Joe Mercer. In the event it was Alf Ramsey, whose tactics never won his approval. If Hogan was among those who were critical of Ramsey's failure to promote wingmanship, he delighted in England's World Cup win and, in any case, he accepted that Ramsey had looked around at the wingers who were available and knew that his choice was limited. He was accused of being a willing victim of the situation. Either way, had anyone taken notice of Hogan, less than a decade before, they would have noted that the art of the winger was fast disappearing. In 1954 he pointed out that in a typical season by January the middle of all League pitches were like ploughed fields while the wings were still covered by grass... not accepting that the basic reason was that more players played in the middle of the field than on the wings, he blamed it on the abandonment of wing play.

When Burnley reached the quarter-finals of the European Cup in the 1960-61 season, the officials of the Hamburg SV side that beat them over two legs presented him with a pennant. They invited him to a local hotel to celebrate and made him Guest of Honour. And in 1967 when Eintracht Frankfurt played Burnley in the Inter-Cities Fairs' Cup at Turf Moor their president, Rudolf Gramlich, took the opportunity to pay a personal tribute to the man he said "forty years ago taught me the arts of the game". Gramlich, a former captain of West

# THE SADNESS

Germany himself, said that more than half of the German team that won the third place play-off in the 1934 World Cup finals had been Hogan's pupils. He added that Hoffman was an example of Hogan's ability to spot a young player and raise him to high international standards.

At that same reception one of football's most cantankerous football administrators of the era, Burnley's chairman Bob Lord, was warm in his praise. "Football in the world has certainly gained from the illustrious career of Jimmy Hogan. We in Burnley are proud that, in his twilight days, he has returned to the nest where he was born, having left his true mark throughout the whole sphere of world football. Well done Jimmy."

While still living in Brunshaw Avenue, he continued to attend many of Burnley's matches as well as travelling around the north simply watching junior football for the pleasure of it, while still taking delight in discovering promising young players. Ron Atkinson recalled that the last time they met "I'm almost certain was at a match at Rochdale, but I can't remember why he was there". Doubtless still doing a little talent spotting for Villa or Burnley.

He continued to give his strong opinions to anyone, from kids he saw playing on the park to Sports Editors, managers and officials, and he was certainly not an old-timer who felt that the modern professional received too much money for too little work. In the late Sixties, as footballers began to be better rewarded, he said he was pleased to see it. He told the Burnley Evening Star: "When you consider what some pop singers are earning I don't see any reason why footballers should not get good wages. I regard footballers as entertainers, the football field as a kind of huge stage. They are entitled to a good salary."

In his 83rd year he seemed less pessimistic about the future of the British game, telling a local newspaper writer: "We are gradually coming back and I would say without doubt that we have more natural footballers in Britain than any country I have worked in. I've looked at the youngsters to prove the point. Give a very young child in this country a ball and it's a safe bet he'll kick it. In the same circumstances on the Continent the child will almost certainly use his hands to catch it. It's bred in us to play football."

Despite all of his years promoting the subtle side of the game he said he was concerned that British players seemed to have lost the art of effective, ball-winning tackling and that there was too much emphasis on the retreating defence. He also complained that there were not enough goals and said that the young players he met did not seem to "live the game as we used to". He was also amazed to find that many of them were not even very interested in talking about it. He was unhappy to hear that many were only too pleased to see the end of their training sessions whereas he said that in his day as a player he never wanted them to end.

The Burnley club continued to make sure that he was around on special occasions. In the 1972-73 season (when they won the Second Division championship) he was invited to Turf Moor to watch a match against Watford and was Guest of Honour for the day. He saw Burnley win, which always made his face and his pipe light up.

# 20

# Recognition at the Last

IN HIS LATE EIGHTIES HE began to deteriorate with the debilitating effects of emphysema which kept him in hospital for several months. He was immensely frustrated because he could not get to matches at Turf Moor. But he had a determined constitution and even after his 90th birthday he was still taking a real interest in football. No longer able to go to games, he was delighted that television could bring them to him. He would chuckle as some of the players of the day failed to trap the ball in the way he had taught and the way he as a player had always found natural. It annoyed him that because of a lack of proper control centre forwards were frequently taking the ball back out of the opponent's penalty area in order to find space to have a shot or play the ball safely out to the wings.

His joy at being able to watch matches on television was a confirmation of a long held belief that League football should be shown live. In fact as early as 1955, when he was still coaching the Villa youngsters in the Warwickshire Combination, he had written in Birmingham's Evening Despatch: "Not very long ago TV was regarded as a menace which would keep thousands of people away from the game and this opinion still prevails. Yet Mr. Arthur Drewry (chairman of the FA) told the recent League meeting that he had often watched TV during his illness and realised that football was losing valuable propaganda that other sports were getting.

# PROPHET OR TRAITOR?

"Look how the popularity of other contests such as boxing, show jumping, tennis, yes, even table tennis, have increased enormously through live transmission. Of course I admit that football draws more crowds than any of these sports. But the football gospel must be spread, and it must be absurd for the League clubs to stop the march of progress.

"Many people who have never seen the game were just fascinated with the football displayed on TV in the World Cup competition. The clubs have a great safeguard in the BBC's willingness to keep the identity of a televised match a secret. And real football supporters will always attend - they wouldn't miss the proper atmosphere for anything. They prefer to be out in the fresh air giving vent to their feelings. Football must concern itself with maintaining the game's popularity, and I believe that television can help it do it."

As failing health began to ask its questions of a man whose active life had allowed him to remain fit for so long, he needed more and more hospital treatment. He hated the idea of dying without recognition in his own country and would not be slow to remind anyone who associated with him that he was "Burnley's most famous football celebrity". Paul Cain, a fellow out-patient, sometimes travelled with him in the ambulance on the way to hospital. He heard a familiar tale. "He told me: 'I am a product of Burnley rec. football. If you can control a ball wearing clogs you can really play the game. Football is played on the floor to keep possession of the ball. When it's played in the air you lose control.'" It made a fitting and familiar epitaph.

James (Jimmy) Hogan died in Burnley General Hospital at the end of January, 1974 aged 91. His son Frank had the task of writing to clubs and national associations all over Europe notifying them of his father's death. Each one contained a personal reference emphasising the nomadic existence he had experienced following his father from country to country. To

# RECOGNITION AT THE LAST

Dresden Sports Club ("I still have happy memories of living in Dresden many years ago"). To Berner Fussball Klub (Berne) ("I still have happy memories of living in Berne"). To Deutscher Turn und Sport Bund ("I still have happy memories of living in Germany"). To The Hungarian FA ("My father had wonderful memories of his time in Hungary working with MTK and was so proud of his name Jimmy Bacsi"). To the Austrian FA ("I still have happy memories of living in Vienna"). To: Racing Club de Paris ("I still have happy memories of living in Paris"). To Lausanne Sports ("I have happy memories of living in Lausanne").

**Dozens of tributes poured in. Among those who wrote were:**

Herr F. Banhalmi (President Magyar Testgyakorlok Kore, MTK): *"He was the founder and master of football in our Sport-Club and we shall pay the tribute of respect to his memory."*

Sir Stanley Rous (President of FIFA): *"I am often asked by people who remember Jimmy in central Europe to give them news and I know that some wrote to him c/o Burnley FC, the only address I could give them. He will long be remembered especially by me who worked with him for many years."*

Helmut Schoen (National Coach of the German Football Federation): *"A few days ago I received the sad news that your father, Jimmy, had passed away at the age of 92 years. Due to the fact that I received the information belatedly, it was not possible for me to attend the funeral. I would like to convey to you that throughout my life I greatly admired your father and always regarded him as a shining example for the coaching profession. The Sport-Club Dresden, where you and your brother played as well, does not exist any more; but the days when your father laid the foundation for the subsequent great success of this club remain alive in our memories. In my lectures to coaches today, I still mention his name frequently, and I know to tell many an interesting anecdote as well. Dear Frank, please rest assured that I and those who knew and regarded him highly will keep fondest memories of your dear father."*

Hans Passblack (Secretary General of the German Football Federation): *"Your father was one of the great personalities of football. His coaching activities are remembered in our country to this very day. The deceased was one of the founders of the teachings of modern football. We have built upon the results of his work and therefore owe him a great deal. You may be certain that we will always keep an honourable memory of your father. Sharing your grief."*

Dr Heinz Geroe (President) and Otto Demuth (General Secretary) of the Austrian FA: *"The outstanding services which Jimmy Hogan rendered to the Austrian Football Association contributed very much to the development of the game in this country. All his Austrian friends will keep a dear memory of Jimmy Hogan and deplore the loss of a great personality in Association Football and of a most kind and charming friend."*

Matt Busby (Director, Manchester United): *"We won't forget to say a prayer for the Great Old Man."*

Bob Lord (Chairman Burnley FC): *"I want you to know that during the last ten or twelve years I became very much attached to your father who in my estimation has been one of the brightest features connected with football during the last*

226

# RECOGNITION AT THE LAST

*thirty or forty years of my life, and his life also. I can assure you that in many phases of football he is very highly known and certainly well respected. You can always carry that in your mind as long as you live. We at Burnley feel we have lost a very sincere friend.*"

Lord also wrote to Hogan's sister Kathleen (Kate) saying: "*He was revered throughout this country of football. Many are the times in my travels when I have been asked did I know Jimmy Hogan. The pride I have felt in being able to truthfully say, yes, has helped me so many times in darker days. Your brother was a person who having been privileged to get to know him was one I looked up to at all times. He has encouraged me to travel the path I had chosen. He never failed to appreciate kindness and he was to me and many others a true reflection of a perfect gentleman.*"

Eric Houghton (Director and former manager of Aston Villa FC): "*I have many happy memories of him with our football days together over several years at Villa Park. He is still held in high esteem by everyone here. He was a great man in every way, and I am very thankful for having had the opportunity of being in football with him for so many happy years.*"

Vic Crowe (Manager Aston Villa FC): "*I think you know that the club really appreciates what your father did for us.*"

Joe Mercer (General Manager Coventry City FC): "*As you know, Jimmy and I were friends for a long, long time. He worked with me during my early days at Aston Villa and contributed a lot to coaching and football in general. He will be sadly missed.*"

# PROPHET OR TRAITOR?

Pepi Liegl (Austrian Football Federation): *"The contents of your letter dated the 31st of January have saddened me deeply. I share in your sorrow; you and your siblings have suffered a great loss. Jimmy was a marvellous, great comrade, full of good-heartedness and always willing to help. Conveying my heartfelt condolences to you, I remain with best regards."*

A Requiem Mass was held at St. Mary's, Burnley and was attended by many famous football personalities including Tommy Docherty (then managing Manchester United). Burnley players Martin Dobson, Keith Newton, Paul Fletcher and Alan Stevenson were the pall bearers. The club was officially represented by Mr. R. Hargreaves (director) and Mr. Albert Maddox (secretary). Two friends of the family, Fr. Harold Cowen and Fr. Frank Myerscough, celebrated Mass. Fr. Myerscough said Jimmy had won respect not only in Burnley but throughout the world.

Jimmy Hogan received greater British recognition in death than he did in life. To their lasting credit, over the years before and after his passing a few British and Continental sportswriters made efforts to record his contribution to football in their articles and books. Geoffrey Green, Ivan Sharpe, Brian Glanville and Hugo Meisl's brother, Willy, were prominent among them.

**He is buried at the Rosegrove Cemetery, Burnley.**

# BIBLIOGRAPHY

The following books were invaluable sources of information:

Association Football (A. H. Fabian and Geoffrey Green) (The Caxton Publishing Company Limited)

Association Football and English Society (Tony Mason) (The Harvester Press)

Back Page Football  (Stephen F. Kelly) (Aurora Publishing)

British Sports Past & Present: Soccer (Denzil Batchelor) (Batsford)

Billy Wright: A Hero For All Seasons (Norman Giller) (Robson Books)

Brian Glanville's Book of Footballers (Puffin Books)

Britain versus Europe (Roger Macdonald, Pelham Books)

Clown Prince of Soccer (Len Shackleton, Nicholas Kaye)

Going For Goal (Peter McParland) (Souvenir Press)

Great Moments in Sport: Soccer (Geoffrey Green) (Pelham Books)

My Twenty Years of Soccer (Tommy Lawton) (Heirloom Modern World Library)

Puskas On Puskas (Rogan Taylor and Klara Jamrich) (Robson Books)

Second To None (John Motson) (Pelham Books)

Soccer: A Pictorial History (Roger Macdonald) (Collins)

Soccer Coaching The European Way (Eric Batty) (Souvenir Press)

Soccer Nemesis (Brian Glanville) (Secker and Warburg)

Soccer Revolution (Willy Meisl) (Phoenix Sports)

Stan Cullis: The Iron Manager (Jim Holden) (Breedon Books)

Soccer The World Game (Geoffrey Green) (Phoenix House Limited)

The Book of Football Quotations (Peter Ball and Phil Shaw) (Stanley Paul)

The Complete Encyclopedia of Football (Keir Radnedge) (Carlton Books Limited)

The Football Managers (Tony Pawson)  (Eyre Methuen)

The Official History of The Football Association (Bryon Butler) (Macdonald  Queen Anne Press)

The Sixty Memorable Matches  (Richard Widdows)  (Marshall

Cavendish Publications Limited)
The Story of Football (Martin Tyler) (Marshall Cavendish Limited)
Tommy Docherty Speaks (Pelham Books)
Tommy Docherty: The ABC of Soccer Sense (B. T.Batsford Ltd)
Tommy Docherty: Soccer From The Shoulder (Stanley Paul)
World Soccer From A to Z (Norman Barrett) (Pan Books Limited)
Stanley Matthews: The Authorized Biography (David Miller)
(Pavilion)

## OTHER SOURCES

Austria Information
Burnley Express
Burnley Evening Star
Daily Record
Deutscher Fussball-Bund
Evening Dispatch (Birmingham)
Hungarian News and Information Service
Nelson Leader
Nelson Library
"Sport"
The Guardian
The Times